Mythanalysis

Mythanalysis

Pierre Solié

Translated by Margaret Jewett
with the assistance of
Ronald G. Jalbert

Chiron Publications • Wilmette, Illinois

Originally published as *Mythanalyse Jungienne.*
Copyright, Les Editions ESF, Paris.

Library of Congress Catalog Card Number: 98-21897

Printed in the United States of America
Copyedited by Carla Babrick and Siobhan Drummond
Cover design by D.J. Hyde

Library of Congress Cataloging-in-Publication Data:
    Solié, Pierre.
        Mythanalysis / Pierre Solié : translated by Ronald Jalbert and
    Margaret Jewett.
            p.   cm.
        Includes bibliographical references (p.   )
        ISBN 1-888602-03-1 (alk. paper)
        1. Myth—Psychological aspects. 2. Symbolism (Psychology)
    3. Psychoanalysis. 4. Jungian psychology. 5. Jung, C. G. (Carl
    Gustav), 1875–1961. I. Title.
    BF175.5.M95S65   1998
    291.1'3'019—dc21   98-21897
                                                        CIP

Contents

Foreword

Mythanalysis? What are we to do with myths? Myths belong to scholars, folklorists, and structuralists. At worst, we can recount myths to children in the same way that we can show them wooden plows and stone-tipped arrows in museums.

Nevertheless, Pierre Solié shows us how myths are active in contemporary life. We find mythological heroes and dramas in the form of people and events we encounter each day. Myths merge with our surroundings and their emotional charge is occasionally released in the body, for better or for worse.

Freud discovered that children, adolescents, and adults unknowingly repeat the peripeteia of the oedipal myth. With this observation in mind, we might assume that myths express the often-paradoxical situations of different moments of human existence. When he broke with Freud, Jung retained Freud's hypothesis about myths and expanded it by commenting on Hiawatha, Cybele, Mithras . . . and especially on Job and Jesus.

In the present book, Pierre Solié continues this tradition by paying particular attention to two myths about the Great Mother that are meaningful to him: those of Tiamat and Isis. He analyzes these myths using several developmental diagrams and proposes the concept of chiasma to account for the crossovers where psychological changes take place. Starting with different data, he thus arrives at the structure of quaternity, which consists of two crisscrossing couples, within which Jung saw the main organizing schema of the psyche. The chiasma is the process by which the quaternity functions.

In this way, myths give us something to think about. Mythanalysis sees myth as the projection of collective unconscious processes, and in this way it contributes to a science of human nature.

For Laura, whose case is presented in chapters 1 and 5, the situation was altogether different. Possessed by a deadly and elusive dynamic, she needed treatment. The use of mythology began when her therapist saw in her personal story an analogy to the Egyptian journey of the dead. The myth bestowed meaning on experiences that seemed meaningless and allowed for conscious work with the unconscious pressure that had until then remained repressed and destructive.

The mere recounting of the myth clearly would not have been sufficient. Therapy additionally offered Laura the four traditional conditions that allow for psychological working through: 1) the narrative, evoked periodically in the therapy; 2) the enactments corresponding to that narrative (in her case study, we see to what extent the patient acted out rather than talked about episodes of self-healing); 3) the privileged space-time, removed from everyday preoccupations, that she found in the analytic session; and 4) the respondent and initiator that her therapist could be because he himself was capable of resonating deeply with the symbolic dimension of the journey of the dead. Insofar as it is a therapeutic activity, mythanalysis releases the dimensions of myth. A living myth entails the enactment of rituals that evoke the successive phases of the story, at a particular time and in a particular space and under the purview of someone who is already an initiate.

Must we conclude from this that the use of such a method is limited to exceptional therapeutic encounters which alone are capable of satisfying the necessary conditions mentioned above? The numerous cases presented as clinical documents in the second part of the book show that this is not the case. We can say even more: the use of myth in therapy often seems essential.

In his book, *Medecines Initiatiques* (1976), Pierre Solié examined the model of the primitive village: a group of huts surrounded by bush and encircling totemic signs that ensure the village's cohesion, unity, and meaning. We are not far removed from such a village when the "bush" consists of job insecurity, the jungle of bureaucracy, and the violence of human relationships. The bush surrounds us, attracts us, overwhelms us. Young adults who enter the social world are fascinated and panicked by it. To become engaged in life, they need inner consistency, which has first to be received from someone else before they can find it for themselves. Identification makes this transition possible.

Ancient myths play this role when contemporary society has no living symbolic order to propose and when parents cannot prevent this deficit. When no one is qualified to tell myths, the task falls to those who function as psychotherapists. When totem poles are overturned, fantasies and passions overtake consciousness, either becoming extremely strong or being pitted one against the other. The therapist's task then is to help the patient find meaning in fragmentation, to discover in it the outline of a potential organization, and finally to allow for necessary differentiation. Myths speak at precisely this level. They represent the experience of these transitions. They tell us what is successful, what fails, and under which conditions success and failure occur. Myths are at once topography, genealogy, and history. The characters and their deeds are linked in sequences that, according to their tendencies, make or undo relationships in the inner and outer worlds. Confronted with cold, hunger, love, birth, and death, humanity has gradually given itself symbols that make it live (Jung 1964).

Jung tells us that

> myth has a "saving," i.e., therapeutic significance, since it gives adequate expression to the dynamism underlying the individual entanglement. The myth is not to be causally explained as the consequence of a personal . . . complex, but should be understood teleologically, as an attempt of the unconscious itself to rescue consciousness from the danger of regression. (1924)

Pierre Solié admirably demonstrates how necessary it is to assume the existence of archetypal mechanisms if relationships between representation and thing, between psychic reality and physical reality, are to be understood. He provides a foundation for the status of the image, whose study he takes up in *Psychanalyse et Imaginal* (1980a).

In observing the power of myth, one is led to discover, in line with Jungian theory, that the image is essentially an organizing schema and that to consider image only as the relationship between signifier and signified is a mistake (Guy-Gillet 1977, pp. 6–17).

In fact, Pierre Solié's book is not merely the presentation of a method. It invites us to reflect on the power of the imaginative life.

In his autobiography, Jung writes:

> The more the critical reason dominates, the more impoverished life becomes; but the more of the unconscious, and the more the myth we are capable of making conscious, the more of life we integrate. Overvalued reason has this in common with political absolutism: under its dominion the individual is pauperized. (1961, p. 302)

Elie G. Humbert

Part One

Mythanalysis Defined

1

Laura's Case, or the Return to the Land of Egypt

In introducing the concept of mythanalysis, it seems best to present a clinical case at the outset, at the risk of offending the rule that stipulates placing methodology before clinical description. We need not be misled by this approach: the clinical case simply enables presentation of the methodology.

Laura was referred to me by her uncle, a psychiatrist colleague and friend. She was twenty-four years old, a student of psychology who was already working in a center for young drug addicts. Rather, she was trying to work, for she was becoming more and more depressed, "empty" to the point that she felt trapped in an abyss inhabited by frightening monsters, depersonalized to the point that she could no longer recognize herself in a mirror. She felt fragmented as well, to such a degree that each internal or external stimulus felt like a piece of herself, separated from all the other pieces and from the world around her. Depersonalized and half in a dream state at certain moments due to the intensity of these phenomena, she was nevertheless conscious of them. Her dreams—daydreams and nocturnal dreams, as both involve the same state of consciousness—revolved around the theme of death and life beyond death.

3

This theme centered on her mother, who had died nine years earlier and for whom Laura's grief—of pathological proportions—was still alive in the form of this loss of soul: emptiness, depression, fragmentation, extreme depersonalization, phobic dreaming, "bad object." Laura's loss of soul alternated with periods of elation, exaltation, contentment, and playful dreaming, in which she managed to rediscover in her fantasies a state of fusion with the "good mother" ("good object"). The absence of the good-object mother immediately sent her back to the bad object. When possessed, through the Imaginary (Lacan 1975, 1977a, 1977b, 1988),[1] by her fantasized mother, whom she saw as concretely real in the past and in the present (beyond death), she was filled with feelings of euphoria. The Imaginary absence of the fantasized mother emptied her and plunged her into the very throes of death and beyond, into a recurrent dream-image of torture beyond death, which explains her endless efforts to rediscover this positive presence within herself. Laura's attempts to avoid such psychic pain were evident in her tight focus on memories, photographs, and mementos and on tape recordings of her mother's voice, as well as in her constant visits to familiar places and a dreamlike journey beyond death.

Laura's father was absent. When ill, he spent the better part of his time painting heads of Christ. A year after the death of his wife, he married his second wife, a friend of the family with whom Laura was unable to establish any deep emotional relationship. What is more, she could not forgive her father; she viewed his new relationship as adultery, a betrayal of her mother. At that point she developed a case of facial acne which resisted all treatment, but which disappeared very quickly after she began therapy. Laura had two younger brothers and a brother and sister who were older.

When she came to see me, she had already consulted several Freudian colleagues. With each of them, she had developed a massive symbiotic transference that was interpreted to her prematurely, aggravating her condition. Eventually she either left them or was gently led away. At the end of our first session, I, like my colleagues, would have gladly sent her out on her own or, worse still, hospitalized her, if I had not been on such good terms with her psychiatrist uncle, to whom I conveyed my impressions and doubts.

During this same period, I was quite captivated by manifestations in myself of what, in C. G. Jung's terms, is called the archetype of the Great Mother goddess, with her son or daughter lovers (Solié 1980b). This personal exploration doubtless was the real reason that I accepted Laura's massive transference. I agreed to dream along with her Imaginary and to experience with her the pathological grieving for her mother. I grieved for her mother and for my own, who also had died when I was eleven years old.

During our third session, Laura's dreamlike discourse particularly attracted my attention. Where had I heard—or read about—this initiatory theme of life beyond death? When I concentrated on this theme and on my memories relating to it, a title suddenly came to mind: "The Book of the Dead." But which one was I thinking of, the Tibetan *Bardo Thodol* or the older Egyptian one?[2] Both of them, no doubt. The fundamental difference between the two is that the *Bardo* imposes on the soul of the deceased the task of releasing itself from the archetypal images that appear and possess it, inducing elation or depression. This release from images is necessary because they are illusions (maya) of the desire (kama) still attached to the things of the world. The forty-nine days of the *Bardo*, an intermediary period between life and complete death, are spent fighting this invasion of the alluring Imaginary: possessive, inquisitive, fusional, and depersonalizing. The soul of the deceased depends on the outcome of this battle. Either it is completely freed from this illusory Imaginary of desire and gains access to the definitive nirvana and satori, or it remains a prisoner of the Imaginary and is once again reincarnated into a fully instinctual body, which it has not been able to abandon. In this case, the cycle of karma (of the necessary redemption) remains unbroken.

As for the Egyptian *Book of the Dead*, it assures us, on the contrary, of the completely objective, nonillusory reality of these archetypal images. The archetypal images are roughly the same in the two systems of life after death: they both deal with grief, initiation, and transcendence of death in the here and now. But according to the *Bardo*, it is appropriate to fight the images in order to rid the soul of them forever, while in the Egyptian *Book of the Dead*, the soul fights them to go beyond them into a spiritual transcendence of the Imaginary. I will call this

5

transcendence the "Imaginal," after Henry Corbin (1960, 1969, 1977, 1996), to distinguish it clearly from the instinctual immanence that Jacques Lacan (1975, 1977a, 1977b, 1988) calls the "Imaginary."

I understood then that the path followed by my Freudian colleagues was the "dry path" of the *Bardo Thodol*, though they did not refer to it as such. Meanwhile, Laura sought the "moist path" of images on which the ancient Egyptians had traveled. She needed to believe in the objective reality of these images of the *Bardo*, of the "intermediary world," of the "twelve pylons (doors) of Osiris."[3] These images could not be erased and disappear like the illusions of the veil of maya. They needed to be metamorphosized from the instinctual Imaginary into the spiritual Imaginal to avoid dragging Laura's suffering soul into infernal emptiness. Never for a moment should these images be abolished to make room for the emptiness of nirvana or of satori.

It was essential that she rediscover her dead mother so she could rediscover her own identity, which had been alienated and dissolved within her mother. She needed to accompany her mother's soul on the journey of the dead and, in particular, pass through the "twelve pylons (doors) of Osiris" to reach the "weighing of souls." The Egyptian dead were judged at that point, either to undergo beatific "Osirinization" or else to be eternally damned to the underworld of Osiris's brother and enemy, Seth. In the form of a monstrous crocodile, Seth awaited the deceased near the scale of Osiris.

Of course, Laura was not even aware of the existence of these books of the dead or of the pre- and post-mortem initiation mythologies that they contain. Since most readers may be equally unaware of them, I am going to give a general sketch of the ancient Egyptians' key ideas of initiation. After that I will turn to the death mythologies of the Akkado-Babylonians, which are still more ancient than those of the Egyptians.

Notes

1. Jacques Lacan's concept of instinctual immanence.
2. In one way or another, every civilization has its own mythology

about death. See *Bardo Thodol* (1957) and *The Ancient Egyptian Book of the Dead* (1966).

3. The twelve hours of the nocturnal life, in the underworld realm where Osiris presided. Osiris was the god of resurrection, as opposed to Seth, the demon of damnation and the negative and monstrous twin brother of Osiris.

2

Myths About Life, Sex, and Death: The Myth of Isis and Osiris

OSIRIS AND HIS WIFE, ISIS[1]—WHO WAS ALSO HIS TWIN sister—reigned over a civilized and unified Egypt. This situation enraged his twin brother, Seth, who hated Osiris with jealous intensity. Along with some conspirators, Seth decided to use a trick to destroy his brother: he had a magnificent and richly decorated treasure chest made to his brother's exact measurements, and then he sent out a challenge, promising this prize to the one who could exactly fit into it. Osiris won the contest by fitting perfectly into the chest. As soon as he lay down in it, however, Seth's conspirators locked the chest's cover over Osiris. They poured lead over the chest and threw it into the Nile to be carried away to the Mediterranean where it would remain forever sunken in the deepest depths of the sea.

When Isis, Osiris's sister and lover, heard the terrible news, she grieved for a long time. Then, though she was still in mourning, she went off to look for him. The first part of Isis's quest led her all the way to Byblos, in Phoenicia. There she discovered the coffer-coffin of her lover buried in the heart of the most beautiful cedar tree in the region. The tree had become the main pillar of the local king's palace (whence the pillar Djed, which came to represent Osiris in future commemorations of his sacrificial initiation). To recover Osiris's body, Isis entered the palace as a nurse for the youngest child of the royal household. She soon attempted to immortalize the child by starving him and placing him in a burning fire. But when the queen caught her doing these things, she was so upset by these acts that she forced Isis to reveal her identity. The goddess then was allowed to claim the pillar for herself and retrieve from it the coffer and the body of her beloved. Isis brought Osiris back to Egypt, but the two sons of the king of Byblos died in the process: the younger from the goddess's loud sobs at the sight of her lover's body, and the older from the goddess's furious glare when he tried to look at Osiris's body in its sarcophagus.

Wishing to visit the house where her son Horus (the Younger) lived, Isis hid her lover's body in some reeds by the Nile. Seth chanced to be hunting in the area that night and found the famous coffer, which he recognized. Incensed, he took his brother's body and cut it into fourteen pieces, which he spread in all directions.

And so began the second phase of Isis's quest, her exhaustive search for the fourteen pieces of her lover. Wherever she found one of these precious remains, there she erected a sanctuary. The fourteenth part of the sacred body of Osiris, however, could not be found because it had been devoured by the fishes of the Nile. That piece was the divine penis. Isis therefore made a copy of it, in erection. She molded it, sculpted it out of every material, anointed and consecrated it, and presented this all-powerful phallus to be venerated in all parts of Egypt. She restored and resurrected the castrated corpse of her lover so that the reborn Osiris became god of the underworld of the second birth (Amenti), while the evil brother, Seth, became the demon of the underworld of eternal damnation (Duat). A strongly symbolic *hieros gamos,* or sacred sexual union, closes the cycle of the sacrificial god's passion.

This cycle is significant from many points of view. It tells us not of an oedipal struggle between father and son for the mother, but rather of a fratricidal struggle for the sister-lover. In fact, Seth should be interpreted as the monstrous double of

Osiris (Girard 1977), his shadow (Jung 1928), and Isis as the mother of the second birth (anima)[2] for Osiris.

We should note that Isis as mother-sister-consort nevertheless retains some characteristics of the incestuous (death) mother of the first birth. The two royal children of Byblos, destroyed by her grief and anger, suggest her responsibility for the two deaths of her brother and son-lover, Osiris. Moreover, she is connected as a double to the goddess Hathor and to her *omophagia* (the eating of bloody live flesh).

Hathor, in a manic state and possessed by her cannibalistic demon, sucked the blood of poor humans every day; they all would have died but for the last-minute intervention of the other gods and goddesses of the Egyptian pantheon. Under the effect of the incest taboo, the Imaginary mother of the first birth becomes a devouring dragon by merging cannibalistic oral drives with possessive genital drives. In the case of Isis, scopophilic drives, in the form of gazing, had a deadly effect on the two royal children of Byblos. Nevertheless, in these predominantly oral dramatizations (cf. the themes of birth and rebirth *per os*) of the Great Mother of the first birth and her son-lover, we are far from the devouring themes of the Babylonian Tiamat and Marduk, her son-lover.[3] For the Egyptians, Isis clearly appears as the mother of the second, or genital, birth: in our own Imaginary, she is identified with the anima. She remains the prototype of all goddesses of mercy, love, and resurrection—including the Christian Virgin who eventually assumed many of these attributes.

Note that the Egyptian passion of Osiris includes four typical stages:

1—Death through the sarcophagus (*sarco-phage*, "meateater").
2—Dismemberment (*diasparagmos*).
3—Castration and the metamorphosis of the penis into a phallus.
4—Resurrection and the emergence of the uterus of the second birth (Amenti).

These stages provide a complete cycle of initiation, emphasizing the metamorphosis of both oral and genital drives.[4] Death through the sarcophagus implies a resurrection, or in any case a re-erection within the heart of the Cedar of Byblos, which symbolizes the Earth Mother's phallus as well as her uterus (heart) of rebirth.

The Djed pillar—which later represents both the phallus and the spinal column of Osiris—and the heart (uterus) of this same pillar form what is called a mythological syzygy, or conjunction: the father, or rather the animus (masculinity) of the mother and the mother herself are fused together. This fusion is what Melanie Klein (1975 and 1984) calls the "fantasy of the combined parents" and what Freud (1914)[5] calls "the primal scene." In this case the syzygy is beneficent because it allows for a rebirth. Usually, though, the syzygy is purely sadomasochistic, especially in its Freudo-Kleinian formulation. The dismemberment (*diasparagmos*) is repaired by the soul sister (anima), but it is nevertheless marked by castration. This sequence demonstrates undeniably the firm link that has united these two initiatory processes since the beginnings of shamanism: dismemberment is linked to orality (we do not devour without first biting) and castration to genitality (we do not transcend the maternal incest of the first birth without the symbolic castration that allows us to reach the soul sister or anima). Castration, insofar as it is a partial sacrifice, constitutes a rite of passage that provides an avoidance and a way out of dismemberment as complete sacrifice (Solié 1980b).[6]

Castration is the event that effects a psychological and sexual chiasma, or crossing-over, between Osiris and Isis.[7] Osiris loses his incestuous, infernal penis of the first birth, and Isis acquires a phallus of rebirth; she gains her animus, her psychological soul and sex that complement her gender.[8] Isis loses her incestuous, infernal uterus of the first birth (through the sacrifice of the two children and Hathor's *omophagia*), and Osiris acquires a uterus of rebirth (at the level of the second birth: Amenti); this uterus of rebirth refers to his anima, his psychological soul and sex that complement his gender. Isis's psyche (soul) is masculinized, Osiris's psyche is feminized. The soul (or *ba*, represented by a hieroglyphic bird and associated with *ib*, a hieroglyphic meaning "heart" and "love") is born to humanity in this myth and achieves a higher level of eros (love). Before, the soul only knew the double (*ka*) and the shadow (*khaibit*). This collective and anonymous "fantasy," formed into myth, is one of the most important ever to emerge from the human Imaginary or Imaginal.

The Ancient Egyptian Book of the Dead

This book[9] comprises verses, incantations, and magic formulae that the deceased had to take along on the great final voyage, in order to cross the menacing thresholds (the pylons of Osiris) of the underworld Duat that leads to the last judgment, or "weighing of souls" (the *ba* and the *ib*). It was well known that the soul and its sins should weigh no more than the feather of Maat, the goddess of cosmic order. The *psychological* sexes, the same sex (double) and the complementary sex (animus and anima), both associated with the heart (*ib*) or love, actually were weighed here. These forces opposed the untamed drives: possessiveness, as in the case of genitality, enslavement, as in anality, and cannibalism, expressed by orality. These three drives had to have been sufficiently metamorphosized into what the Greeks and Romans called respectively eros (the most intimate love), caritas (love of one's neighbor) and agape (universal or cosmic love). These metamorphoses were supposed to reach completion, or at least continue to evolve, during the journey through the intermediary world, as in the case of the Tibetan *Bardo*. Little by little, the soul and the heart were supposed to separate from the body and the instinctual drives. They needed gradually to abandon the archetypal images attached to the body and to desire (the instinctual Imaginary) in order to transcend into archetypal images of soul and spirit (the spiritual Imaginal). Inversely to what occurs in the *Bardo Thodol*, if the deceased were unable to complete this process, they became lost forever in the cosmic void.

The Egyptians were a concrete and materialistic people, bon vivants, comparable to modern-day Americans. Nevertheless, they were preoccupied with the problem of death to the utmost degree. This preoccupation has led some to call the Egyptian mythology of death a "schizophrenic delirium." On close examination, however, their mythology of death is no more delirious or unreal than any other mythology relating to life and death. It certainly has little to do with the "dry path" and the negative theology referred to earlier. On the contrary, it consists of a "moist path" and a multiplicity of archetypal images. These images probably became necessary to the Egyptians because of their inherent extraversion of libido, as pointed out above, as opposed to the introversion of Buddhism (Jung 1921), which stood against the rich tradition of images in Hinduism.

The Egyptian *Book of the Dead* reveals a body of knowledge that we would qualify today as psychosomatic and psychogenetic. The book constituted, in sum, their psychology and their psychoanalysis. The ancient authors differentiated first the physical body, which underwent mummification, the operation necessary to extract the psychospiritual principles that follow during the intermediary journey. This body is an object of contemplation and meditation. It binds the deceased to the Earth, that place where the barge weighed anchor at the person's incarnation. The body is a passive instrument, but one that provides a stable form for the other principles.

Afterward comes the *ka*, the double who, beyond death, plays the role that the physical body played during life. The *ka* is the place of absolute stability, the most condensed and resistant part of the invisible being; it is akin to the Hindu *prana* and the alchemist's *coagula* (sulfur). It resembles the physical body in every way, except that it is immaterial. We would call it the psychological sex double, closely related to animus and anima. It is a centrifugal cosmic ego, as opposed to the centripetal empirical ego. Mummification, as well as the erection of an effigy of the deceased, were necessary to assure its cohesion. Although immaterial, the *ka* still required food during the intermediary journey through the Duat (underworld).

The *khaibit*, or shadow, was the substratum of all instincts, needs, and desires, but also of their aberrations, of all vices and perversions. It is the negative shadow of the double and/or of the complement. Given its corrupt state, it encountered great dangers in the beyond: being destroyed, devoured, or stolen away (as in the shamanic theft of the soul). It is the *khaibit* that appears in the form of disturbing ghosts.

The *ba* (soul) is the twin of the *ib* (heart). In hieroglyphics, it is represented as a bird with a human head. It is the seat of rebirth in the presence of Osiris ("Osirinization"), or of the second and final death, swallowed then by the serpent Apopis, an instrument of Seth. Apopis haunts the visions of the deceased during the intermediate period and occupies a huge place in the labyrinths of the Duat (the underworld of redemption, a purgatory, or of damnation and the second death). The *ba/ib* is endowed with prodigious dynamism and can run the whole gamut of metamorphoses. In this we are reminded of the *solve*, the alchemist's mercuries.

The *khu* (or *iakhu*) is the chosen one, the perfect one, the initiate, very close to the spirit. It already resides in the Fields of Reeds and Peace in the Kingdom of the Dead Reborn (Amenti), far from the Duat of redemption or damnation.

Finally, there is the *sahu*, the body now glorious and blissful, the spirit illuminated and consecrated. We could compare this to the Hindu bodhi and atman, the micro- and macrocosmic Self.

Neither the *khu* nor the *sahu* could ever be attained after the second death. Thus they no longer needed funeral offerings or prayers, incantations or magical formulae. They remained with Osiris for all eternity.

Notes

1. See Plutarch, "On Isis and Osiris," in his *Morals*. Many editions are available, and most abridged editions include this story.

2. We will study this later.

3. See Plutarch, "On Isis and Osiris."

4. Anal drives are definitely only a byproduct of oral drives. If cannibalism of the other and/or of the self is attached to orality, then enslavement is attached to anality and possessiveness to genitality.

5. Especially in his discussion of the Wolf Man. See Freud (1914).

6. The sacrifice of the god who served as son-lover to the Phrygian Great Goddess, Cybele, elaborates this concept. See Solié (1980b).

7. Like the sex cells at meiosis. To imagine this phenomenon, consider the optic chiasma of the pyramids that cross over inside the encephalus.

8. Budge tells us that Isis is represented in the *Book of the Lower World* with a phallus in the form of a knife because "she possesses virility."

9. See Champdor (1963), Kolpaktchi (1979), Mayassis (1961), and Rossiter (1979).

3

Dialectical Models: Cannibalism and Agape

F<small>ORTY-FIVE HUNDRED YEARS AFTER THE</small> E<small>GYPTIAN MYTH</small> of Isis-Osiris, with its messages about death and grieving, Laura presented me with a psychogenesis of pathological grieving that resembled melancholy. Yet more remains to be discovered in her case than merely a psychogenetic melancholia, which, according to Melanie Klein, is a psychogenesis of the "depressive position" attempting to integrate the earlier "paranoid-schizoid position." The Egyptian myths pertain to psychogenesis, plain and simple, in addition to their clear historical relevance. They relate not only to psychogenesis, but even to a therapeutic method by which a deviation, stagnation, or fixation of that psychogenesis can be healed. Besides explaining the classic psychogenesis of childhood and adolescence, the myth of Isis and Osiris further explains the psychogenesis of the second half of life: the spiritual evolution of "Being-Toward-Death" (Heidegger 1959, 1962), the movement toward and in anticipation of death in the present and the attainment of the greatest transcendence, serenity, freedom, and completion in the here and now.

The myth of Isis and Osiris, as well as all other mythologies of death applied to the life of the living, plainly asserts that we are never finished with our earthly body, our instincts, our needs, our desires: in a word, with our drives. All of this is evident, one is tempted to say. But not so fast. Consider Freud's classic theory of psychogenesis, which is quite convenient, eloquent, and close to psychobiological reality, with its three stages (or phases or positions) of orality, anality, and genitality. The outline of psychospiritual evolution contained in the Egyptian mythology of death shows us being forced to return incessantly to these primal psychobiological stages.

This continual return is necessary if we are to alter, gradually and to the extent possible, whatever is wild, brutal, animalistic, inhuman, *homo homini lupus*, about those stages—if we are to move beyond oral cannibalism, anal slavery, and genital possessiveness. Only a difference of degree exists between cannibalistic devouring of the alter ego and possessive control over the genital sexual object. In either case, incorporation of the other is at issue. What is commonly called love has its source in primitive cannibalistic incorporation or introjection. All the great religions and myths are religions of love, because they all strive to metamorphosize this fundamental instinct. In that sense, all religions that deal with the "heart" are cannibalistic.

We will probably never know whether *Homo sapiens neanderthalensis* was generally a cannibal, any more than we are as *sapiens-sapiens*, or any more than the Paleolithic or Mesolithic human might have been. All we know about these ages of humanity is that "cannibalism certainly existed here and there, but the demonstration of its religious character is illusory" (Leroi-Gourhan 1976). And yet we do know of several ethnological tribes who practice religious cannibalism today. Furthermore, all the great myths of origin include a fundamental phase of cannibalism, which has been shown in reference to the Babylonian Great Mother Tiamat. Cannibalism is also evident in Hathor, the Egyptian sacred cow who practiced vampirelike *omophagia*. We have further noted cannibalism as it pertains to the dismemberment (*diasparagmos*) of Osiris. We know that the Greek Uranus sent his children back into the infernal belly of his wife, the Earth Mother Gaia, and that his son Cronus had at least the courage to devour them himself. We could spend quite some time enumerating all the myths in which divine cannibalism comes to light.

We know from other sources (Lévi-Strauss 1963, 1969,

1983) that prohibitions against cannibalism and incest form the foundation of culture and society. Instituting a magic or religious ritual directed at a primal drive implies two essential ideas:

1—The drive is forbidden to the whole social group.
2—The drive can be satisfied, under certain well-defined conditions (transgression *within* the law), by all or a portion of the group membership, who represent at that time the whole group.

The ritual functions to prevent an immediate, wild, and thorough acting out of the drive. Where cannibalism is practiced, it is generally forbidden for members of a tribe to eat each other. Periodically, though, a sacrificial meal will bring all the members of the tribe together with the sacrificer to partake ritually (by transgression within the law) of one of their own (endocannibalism) or of someone from a neighboring tribe (exocannibalism) who has died naturally or by sacrifice.

At such a meal, the oral drive, which has the inherent purpose of conserving the individual's life and which is quick to consume by using all the aggression at its command, can be satisfied through ritualized transgression. This ritual implies a meaning that far transcends simple nutrition: eating the alter ego here means more than assuaging one's hunger for food. Beyond the nutritional goal and object, there is instead a metaphorical-metonymic goal and object defined by continuity and contiguity: to satisfy the hunger for the alter ego, which we can define as the hunger for love. Love at this level means incorporating the other by devouring him or her (as in *diasparagmos* and *omophagia*), thereby appropriating his or her physical and moral qualities. It means making that person our own, completely our own, assimilating the victim even into the depths of our cells. Ultimately, the other ceases to exist—the other has become "flesh of our flesh."

Looking at everyday behavior is enough to remind us how much our love is still bound to the oral register, that is, to cannibalism. Consider a mother kissing her child. "I could eat you up," she says to the child, over and over, without hesitation. The child, who is literally a little cannibal at her breast, reflects this image right back to her. Let us also consider two passionate young lovers. They devour each other with their eyes, with

19

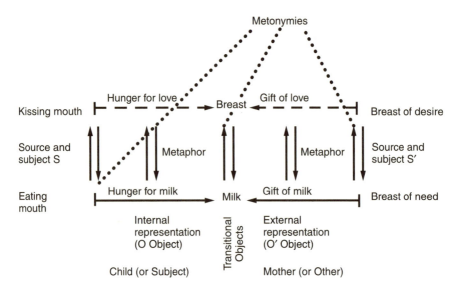

Figure 1

The child's oral drive is linked to the mother's nursing instinct. Below, we see the biological *underpinnings of the drive (physical need). Above, we see the* psychological *superstructure (desire, eros, love) of the same drive. Below, on the side of the child taken as subject, the eating mouth, the hunger for milk and the* internal *representation of this milk; on the side of the mother taken as object or Other (alter ego), the breast of need, the gift of milk and the* external *(objectal) representation that the child acquires of this milk.*

glances as intense as those that Isis directed toward the older child of Byblos. Genital possessiveness still has its roots in the oral register, and this is even more true for anal slavishness. There is a constant metaphorical-metonymic slide from oral and anal libido toward genital libido. The shift from hunger for milk to hunger for love constitutes in effect a metaphorical analogy, while the erotization of the eating mouth first into the kissing mouth and then into the speaking mouth, constitutes a metonymic contiguity. Figure 1 displays these relationships.

The internal representation of the drive object basically points to the potential for the drive object to be represented, in the same way that, for the eye, sight is merely a potential for seeing if there is no light—the external physical force which can realize the eye's potential. Similarly, the external and physical representation of the milk and of the mother's breast is necessary for the realization of the child's internal representation of the instinctual object.

When this internal representation is realized, an engram of this image-object has been produced in the corresponding neocortical DNA of the child. The child has experienced what ethologists today call an imprint, which is as indelible as the imprint of an external object on a photographic plate. At the same time, consider that a child's brain is not a clean slate. If the external image-object is necessary to produce this engram or imprint, the internal potential image-object is equally necessary. Light can always shine; if the living optic system is not there to perceive it, the light shines without knowing that it shines. The optic system is the "signifier" of the light and of all objects that it illuminates, which are the "signifieds."

It is not acceptable, then, to confuse the two image-objects or representations. For the child, the internal image-object is innate, while the external image-object is acquired. It is from the meeting of the two that the representation of "thing," then of "word," is born. The innate internal image-object is already a potential representation—a psychological system inherent in the physiological system of the instinct. The acquired external image-object only stimulates and actualizes what is already there as a potentiality. Without what is already there, nothing happens.

Moreover, what is already there at the beginning of life overpowers what is to come: the external image-object and the perceptual representation that we call objective. The child's perception, like that of an archaic human, is at first subjective: the phenomenologist would say "intrasubjective," the philosopher would say "solipsistic," the psychiatrist would say "autistic" and/or "interpretive." What this means is that the internal image-object projects itself onto the external image-object and eliminates it. This projection is what is commonly called mistaking desires for reality. At this stage, the two objects, internal and external, fuse, with preeminence given to the internal. In other words, the pleasure (or displeasure) principle predominates over the reality principle.

Little by little, reality begins to intrude on the child's world: the breast and the mother's milk are not given continuously, but in general only every three hours. From then on, the child begins to distinguish two realities: his own, which is internal, intrasubjective, and psychic, and that of his mother, which is external, intersubjective, and physical. The two image-objects are separated and split into psychic reality and physical reality. What Freud calls "hallucination of the lost object" is none other than the realization of this psychic reality, potentially already there and primitively hallucinated onto objective physical reality. Thereafter, psychic reality is truly realized; it is distinct from physical reality. Psychic reality is now an engram in the cortex, and it forms what we call the O image-objects, which are correlatives to the image-objects of physical reality while being clearly distinct from them. The image-objects of physical reality, which also are imprinted as engrams, are called O'. O and O' are correlatives. No longer fused or split, from here on they are joined to each other (*coniunctio*).

This bridge between psychic reality and physical reality constitutes, quite literally, a symbol. *Sym-bolon* means to make a bridge or junction. The symbol thus decodes a message inscribed on the two realities that had previously been either separated or fused. This process actually is much like the one used to decode a message when only half of it is available. The conjunction of O and O' constitutes a third term in the dialectic. In this way, one realizes that the objects O and O' are what phenomenologists call noematic objects (Husserl 1950, Sartre 1936–1956 and 1940, Merleau-Ponty 1962). They form the substratum of representations, knowledge, meaning, and finally language. The first, the object O, arises from objective psychic reality that has been incarnated, or become an engram within an individual: it has, in effect, become subjectivized. The other, the object O', comes from objective physical reality that has also been incarnated in an individual or, again, become subjectivized.

In figure 1, the milk and breast that mediate (or "un-fuse") the relationship between the child subject and the mother object are analogous to what Winnicott (1985) calls transitional or intermediary objects. The shift from milk to breast, like the shift from eating mouth to kissing mouth, constitutes a metonymic contiguity. The shift from hunger for milk to hunger for love, like the one from the gift of milk to the gift of love, constitutes a metaphoric analogy. Clearly, these shifts are also reversible.

The images of objective, imprinted psychic reality (O objects) are the foundation for the Imaginary (*eidos*, eidolon), particularly when they fuse with external objects and imbue them with their own intrasubjective meaning.[1] Images of imprinted objective physical reality (O′ objects) are the foundation for the symbolic (*noos*, noetic), which can in turn subsume the Imaginary by superimposing a geometric or legalistic grid over it whereby things are only what them seem. In the first situation, one has an overabundance of signifiers without signifieds, while the opposite holds true in the second situation. Autistic delirium demonstrates the consequences of overabundant signifiers, while interpretive delirium shows us an overabundance of signifieds, though the distinction between the two is not that simple. Lacan's symbolic order is formed from the conjunction of the "eidetic-noematic" correlatives O and O′, which are linked together in a signifying chain. The imaginal register transcends the imaginary and symbolic orders, since the overabundance of signifiers in objective psychic reality (O objects) has not yet been correlated with the signifieds in objective physical reality (O′ objects). In this way, the imaginal order spearheads the search for meaning: one could say that all mythological (archetypal) images are manifestations of the Imaginal.

The masculine soul (animus) born to Isis from the castrated penis of Osiris, just like the feminine soul (anima) born to Osiris from the castration of the toothed uterus or vagina of Isis, as well as the corresponding doubles of Osiris and Isis, all manifest the Imaginal at the heart of the Egyptian myth. What we see there is a new form of (metaphorical-metonymic) "erotization," the emergence of a new knowledge, of a new meaning for humanity and the universe. That is why the apparent unreality of the myth and the notorious unreality of delirium should not be put into the same basket.

Image-objects that come from objective physical reality differ depending on whether they are equipment objects or alter ego objects. In the case of the alter ego object, what is O′ for me is O for another person. Our schema could also very well be reversed if we took the mother as subject and the child as object or other. It is at that level that the phenomenological concept of intersubjectivity acquires its value. Nevertheless, any equipment object as form always remains far removed from the alter ego. In

23

fact, we and the equipment object are fundamentally constituted from the same objective physical reality: particles, atoms, molecules, simple and composed bodies. Without that common fundamental structure, we would have no possibility of recognizing an object or each other: what Jung calls archetype unites psyche and soma, spirit and matter.

Two new schemas (figures 2 and 3) will help us to visualize these phenomena better.

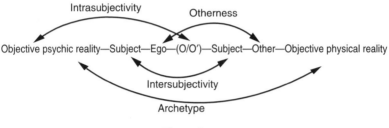

Figure 2

Through alterization, it is the Other (the imaginary mother and her animus, the combined parents, the primal scene, the syzygy of origin) who carries the weight of responsibility. Here we have a typical paranoid-schizoid dialectic (in Klein's terms) involving relationships from the oral-anal world: eater-eaten, aggressor-aggressee, master-slave. The Other is the carrier of the murderous and archaic aspects of the cannibalistic drive.

This way of understanding the child's original relationship to the world approaches Nietzsche's "will to power," which consists of putting down the other as though it were a thing and deriving pleasure from it. To get at the core of sadomasochism, one only needs to add what thing it is that gives pleasure: that other thing is precisely the other subject, or the alter ego. In fact, in putting the other subject down we incorporate it. By cannibalizing and enslaving it, we simply bring it back to the same: we refuse to acknowledge differences, we refuse separation, we refuse the Other. We attempt to conserve "primary narcissism," which culminates in fantasies of incestuous intrauterine bliss. But in so doing, we condemn ourselves to the toothed vagina (*vagina dentata*) of Hathor and to the castrating and dismember-

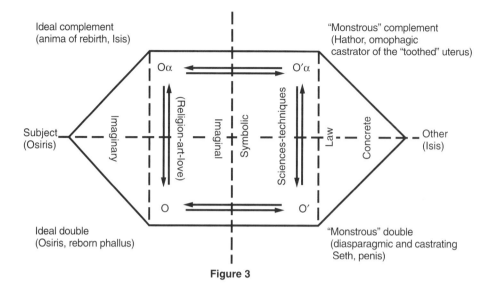

Figure 3

This schema illustrates the Manichean split of "good" and "bad" objects which characterizes Laura's dream life, as well as the Egyptian myth that we have just retraced. It represents Klein's paranoid-schizoid and depressive (as well as maniacal) positions. To the objects O and O' here are added the objects Oα and O'α. In fact, we recognize in these last two what we have already defined as the psychological sexual complements (animus and anima), both ideal (Isis for Osiris and Osiris for Isis) and monstrous (Hathor the vampire and Isis as the murderer of children). To the objects O and O' we give here the mythological correlates: 1) the ideal psychological sex double corresponding to Osiris, reborn and 2) the monstrous double corresponding to Seth the murderer. At this level, it is always the Other who is wrong. The destructive drives are attributed to him by means of projection or "alterization." O'α and Oα can be integrated to create the conjunctions O-O' and Oα-O'α because they are carriers of the diasparagmic (dismemberment) and omophagic (vampirelike) sides of the oral drive. Original untamed cannibalism, and not the cannibalism ritualized within the law, still reigns supreme.

ing penis associated with Seth. Psychogenetic law, however, is such that this pleasure is quickly transformed into the hellish tortures that we have described unless it becomes fixated into sadistic perversion.

The masochistic/depressive phase follows when we acknowledge to ourselves and own the sadism that had previously been attributed to the other. Owning sadism means first turning it against oneself until a metamorphosis comes about. The passion of a god consists in the suffering (or pathos) that results from the potential reversal of sadism into eros. The dialectic of the conjunction between O and Oα on the one hand and between O′ and O′α on the other will only work when Osiris (*patiens*, the sufferer) and Isis (*agens*, the actor) have completed their cycle of sadomasochistic redemption. The dialectic will only work when they have recognized, experienced, and transformed the sadomasochism that is still attached to their relationship to the world (founded instinctively on the cannibalism and slavery of their shadow or *khaibit*, represented here by Seth and Hathor). After this redeeming passion, Seth, the dismemberer or castrator, and Hathor, the vampire woman, become the lawgiving and tutelary agencies that Freud calls superego and ego ideal.[2]

The introjection or incorporation of the law and spirit of the group occurs when law and spirit are ritualized: when a symbolic transgression within the law takes place. All those initiated into the mysteries of Osiris symbolically lived out this passion: through ritual they effected a metamorphosis of their double (*ka*), their shadow (*khaibit*), their soul (*ba*) and their heart (*ib*) to attain the levels of initiate, perfect one (*iakhu*), and, eventually, spirit (*sahu*) and their name of initiate (*ren*). At this point, if we are to be thorough, we must construct another diagram (figure 4).

Jung's "objective psyche," which he also calls the "collective unconscious," is made up of archetypes and is none other than our own psychic objective reality which, when incarnated (O objects) in an individual, leads to what Jung calls the personal or individual unconscious.[3] Consequently, it is not the images that are innate but simply the potential for realizing them, which is actualized through contact with physical reality (the concrete mother and father). What is given is the mold from which images are produced: this is the archetype that links internal and external realities (see figure 2).[4] Thus the archetype of the "combined parents united in uninterrupted, sadistic intercourse" (Klein), with which the child colludes and by which it is thus destroyed, gives form to this syzygic representation. It is a cosmogonic and anthropogonic representation of origin, for which each civiliza-

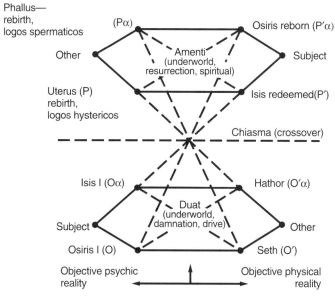

Figure 4
(Intersection of Pyramids)

In this diagram we see Osiris I and Isis I at the level below the crossover (chiasma). They are designated in this way before the drama of their passion and redemption begins, at the point when they are trapped by their sadomasochistic instincts (in the underworld of damnation, Duat), which are represented respectively by Seth (the monstrous double of Osiris) and Hathor (the monstrous double of Isis).

It is these monstrous doubles that are designated by the words "syzygy of origin"—for Klein the "combined parents," for Freud the "primal scene." According to Klein, as well as Freud, we really are talking about an inherited (innate) Imaginary that consequently converges with Jung's innatist concept of the archetype. In fact, it is not the images that are inherited, but only the potential to produce them (or realize them). We have referred to this potential as objective psychic reality and its O objects, at the time the subject comes in contact with the concrete mother and father, which in turn we have called objective physical reality and its O′ objects.

tion has its own eidetic representations (representations in images). The author and thus the general themes are common to all civilizations, but not the director or the actors, or even the more specific themes. The myth of Osiris and Isis is an anthro-

27

pogony because humanity thereby attains a new threshold of soul and heart, of psyche and eros. The Babylonian myth of Tiamat-Apsu is a cosmoanthropogony because from this "sadistic oral intercourse" the universe is born, and with it, humanity. The Greek myth of Gaia and Uranus, which is also oral, thematically is another cosmoanthropogony. These themes are discernible in all the great founding myths of civilization.

While the psychic and physical realities are the same everywhere, the O and O′ objects that they produce vary according to the civilization. Thus it is that Seth, in the Egyptian anthropogony, plays an analogous role to that of the Babylonian Apsu, who plots the destruction of all his descendants, or to that of the Greek Uranus, who sends his children into Tartarus, the infernal belly of his wife Gaia. These myths are not concerned with a paternal but with a fraternal principle. The so-called "precocious oedipal" rivalry (which is in fact preoedipal and pregenital, because it is oral-anal) has little to do with the father (the archetypal image of the Father), but much with the brother (the archetypal image of the Brother, who is here a twin). The same applies, strictly speaking, to the archetypal image of the Mother.

That is why when referring to this level of origins we, along with Jung, prefer to speak of the masculine principle (Apsu, Uranus, and others) as contained within the maternal principle. In other words, we are speaking of the incorporated animus rather than of the "penis of the father incorporated in the mother" (in Klein's terms). The separation, or differentiation, of these two principles, which originally had been confused, constitutes the psychic work of early infancy. Both the early infancy of humanity, phylopsychogenesis, and that of the individual child, ontopsychogenesis, are wholly concerned with making this differentiation, a differentiation between masculine and feminine principles, which furthermore need to be differentiated from the concrete mother and father. It is appropriate to speak of the Imaginary as long as these principles remain fused and confused with each other and with the concrete parents. We can begin to speak of the symbolic when these principles have been differentiated by means of passionate ritualization (diasparagmic and castrational). We can refer to the Imaginal after that, during the individuation (Jung) which occurs in the second half of life when we are confronted with the anticipation of death. In our schema, this last step corresponds to the level above the chiasma.[5]

At the earlier stage below the chaisma, Osiris and Isis have no conscious idea that Seth and Hathor represent their own pre-genital sadomasochism, just as the infant, living in a paranoid-schizoid position, confuses its own sadomasochistic drives with the "bad breast" of the mother, then with the "bad mother" as a whole.[6] Only when the child reaches the depressive position does it begin to be conscious of its responsibility for this phe-nomenon of "badness." We can even say that this ray of con-sciousness is what brings on the depressive position (the Fall). It is then that, for the child, the passionate suffering of the son god emerges, just as the entire history of religion has taught us.

Marduk, the Babylonian son god, is in this way an even bet-ter example than the Egyptian son god Osiris. In fact, as is told during the Babylonian festival of the new year (in March and April), Marduk was put to death by Kingu, an enemy brother and successor of Apsu, who represents here the masculine prin-ciple (animus). Marduk was then absorbed into the Great Mother Tiamat and descended to the underworld, that is to say, into Tiamat's womb (or Tartarus). (This scene constitutes the endocannibalistic incest of the first birth.) There, for three days, he battled against his (archetypal) Great Mother; that is, against oral incest (endocannibalism). At the end of this combat, as the Babylonian creation poem (the "Enuma Elish") tells it, his soul sister (anima) Zarpanitu, also descended into the underworld. There she bandaged him, consoled him, nourished him, healed him, and finally resurrected him. At that point a *hieros gamos* took place, consummating a brother-sister incest (of the second birth), a genital incest radically opposed to the original canna-balistic incest.

The level above the chiasma in the myth of Osiris corre-sponds to the underworld of the second birth (Amenti), which is opposed to the underworld of the first birth (Duat). This means that the level above the chiasma is opposed to the devouring belly of the original syzygy, an underworld of eternal damnation. There we find Osiris, who is reborn but castrated of the incestu-ous penis of the first birth, and Isis, redeemed but with her in-cestuous uterus of the first birth similarly removed. In this ver-sion of the passion, Isis's redemption occurs through that of

29

Osiris. Consider the passive (passion, *patiens*) side of the son god and the active (*agens*) side of the daughter goddess. Osiris seems to suffer more, but we should note that he suffers unconsciously. Isis apparently suffers less, but with full consciousness of her state. This psychogenetic schema is androgynous, and it applies just as much to the girl's psychogenesis as to the boy's. If we take the case of Osiris as the subject of the passion, Osiris I would generally be the ego ideal and Seth the monstrous double (the mother's animus, then eventually the father); Isis I would generally be the ideal complement (anima) and Hathor her monstrous complement (the devouring mother, then eventually the anima of the father). Once reborn, Osiris would be the new ego ideal (the *iakhu*, the perfect one, the initiate), enhanced by the phallus of rebirth, which we call *logos spermaticos* (Solié 1980b).

And now if Isis is taken as the subject of the passion, Isis I would generally be the ego ideal and Hathor her monstrous double (the devouring mother, then eventually the anima of the father); Osiris I would generally be her ideal complement (animus), and Seth her monstrous complement (the mother's animus, then eventually the father). Redeemed, Isis would be the new ego ideal (*iakhu*) enhanced by the uterus of rebirth (*logos hystericos*), and the reborn Osiris would be the new ideal complement (animus) enhanced by the phallus of rebirth (*logos spermaticos*). The chiasma, or the point where the pyramids intersect, is formed by the interweaving of instinctive and spiritual inversions and reversals. It suggests a *somation* (a somatic, rather than a genetic, sexual mutation of the germen) of the neocortical DNA in the course of the sacrificial passion. In this scenario, the sacrifice that has been agreed to—voluntarily if possible, or else by force—of the sadomasochistic-cannibalistic, slavish, or possessive drives, translates into a new genetic arrangement of the chromosomes in the neurons. This new arrangement might have something in common with the chromosomes crossing over during meiosis, when the two gametes (the father's and the mother's) exchange their genetic material. Here, then, is the true feminization of Osiris (his anima of the second birth, his uterus of rebirth, in which to carry the initiates and the deceased to eternal life), as well as the masculinization of Isis (her animus of the second birth, her phallus reborn through her efforts, which demonstrates her power—or potency—in resurrection).

Consequently, Osiris loses his untamed male power (his splitting, violent—and violating—penis) to gain a compassionate femininity (anima). Isis loses her untamed female power (her toothed, omophagic uterus) to gain a reviving and protective masculinity (animus). However, Osiris's reborn ego ideal remains a masculine principle in which eros wins out over hubris (uncontrolled violence); Isis's redeemed ego ideal remains similarly unchanged. Both constitute a principle of eros, masculine and feminine, which unites with the principle of logos, also masculine (*spermaticos*) and feminine (*hystericos*). It is by a crossing over, horizontally rather than vertically, that the reborn Osiris unites with the *logos hystericos*, making from it an eros-logos (Solié 1980a). The redeemed Isis unites with the *logos spermaticos*, making from it a logos-eros (ibid.). Eros-logos and logos-eros are the "spirit guides."

The chiasma appearing in our schema and constructed from the mythanalysis of Osiris and Isis confuses the passionate and instinctual metamorphoses of childhood, specifically those that relate the thresholds of the pregenital, oral-anal, and genital phases with those of adolescence (concerned with initiation into adulthood) and full maturity (concerned with anticipation of death in the here and now). This confusion is justified because the mechanism necessary for metamorphosis is the same at each life stage, but it nevertheless is appropriate to differentiate these stages from each other.

Notes

1. "Inanimate objects, do you then have a soul / Which attaches itself to our soul and forces it to love?"—or to hate.

2. I call these the phallus of rebirth, or *logos spermaticos*, and the uterus of rebirth, or *logos hystericos*; we will return to these concepts.

3. We have seen that the individual unconscious is formed and actualized in the dialectic of the two realities—psychic and physical—and that there is no cortical inscription (imprint or engram) of O objects without the participation of O' objects.

4. Which would explain the phenomena that Jung designates under the term *synchronicity*: a psychic phenomenon and a physical phenomenon that arise simultaneously without any causal link, but that have a

common meaning. Synchronicity appears as coincidence or exaggerated chance.

5. The denominations then become (P-P′) (Pα-P′α); later on we will see why.

6. Note that this means evidently the objective, concrete "bad breast" and "bad mother."

4

The Babylonian Myth of Marduk and Tiamat

The Oral-Genital Chiasma I

This myth depicts the son god Marduk going through two phases: first, a "solar" phase, which is paranoid-schizoid and properly oral; second a "lunar" phase, which is depressive and more clearly anal, approximating the passive suffering evident in the myth of Osiris.

The Solar Hero: The Oral-Anal Chiasma

In the beginning there was the Water Mother, the newly emerged earth, in a state of *massa confusa* or chaos (Garelli and Leibovici 1959). She gives birth to two principles: the masculine principle, Apsu, and the feminine one, Tiamat. Tiamat, however, is masculine above and feminine below. She is chaos, fetus—in cosmic dimensions, she is the embryo of the world. She is depicted as a camel without horns or tail, or a gigantic serpent. In this precosmogonic chaos, she created the gods, or the demons, of the underworld, in particular Anu and Ea.

Ea, in turn, gives birth to Marduk. Apsu (whose procreative role is not explicit, but which must surely consist of "uninterrupted intercourse" or fusion), one day complains to Tiamat that their children are disturbing his eternal bliss. He wants to destroy them. But the omniscient Ea is vigilant and, taking the initiative, it is she who destroys her infanticidal father. Tiamat then decides to avenge her husband by bringing his plan to fruition. Toward this end, she creates monsters:

> monster serpents, sharp of tooth and not sparing the fang. With poison instead of blood she fills their bodies. Ferocious dragons she clothed with terror, so that their bodies might leap forward and none turn back their breasts. She set up the viper, the dragon, and the sphinx, the great lion, the mad dog, and the scorpion-man, driving storm demons, the dragonfly, and the bison, bearing unsparing weapons, unafraid of battle. (Babylonian Genesis 1951, p. 31, tablet 2, 24–34)

Choosing among her firstborn children, she exalts Kingu. She marries him and makes him chief of this infernal army. Anu leads the defense, but he turns back in terror at the sight of the monstrous horde confronting him. Only Marduk agrees to take on the army of the Great Mother.

He goes out to battle alone, taking for his only weapons the four winds, a bow and arrows, and a net. He approaches the army to determine Kingu's intentions, and with the first glance he casts toward the enemy, Kingu faints and falls. The infernal army goes down with him. The way is then clear to approach Tiamat herself, who insults Marduk. Marduk replies

> "the sons treat their fathers unjustly; thou, their bearer, dost hate them without cause. Thou hast exalted Kingu to be thy spouse; thine illegal authority thou hast set up in place of the authority of Anu . . . Come forth alone and let us, me and thee, do single combat!" . . . They pressed on to single combat, they approached for battle. The Lord spread out his net and enmeshed her. The evil wind, following after, he let loose in her face. When Tiamat opened her mouth to devour him, he drove in an evil wind, in order that she should not close her lips. The raging winds filled her belly; her belly became distended, and she opened wide her mouth. He shot off an arrow, and it tore her interior; it cut through her inward parts, it split her heart. When he had subdued her, he destroyed her life; he cast down her carcass and

stood upon it. After he had slain Tiamat, the leader, her band broke up, her host dispersed. . . . He split her open like a mussel into two parts; half of her he set in place and formed the sky as a roof. . . . The lord measured the dimensions of the Apsu, and a great structure, its counterpart, he established, namely Esharra[1], the great structure Esharra which he made as a canopy. . . . In the very center thereof he fixed the zenith.[2]

Now let us turn to what Klein has to say about the child's fantasy of the combined parents. In this fantasy, the child hallucinates that

the penis inside the mother represents a combination of father and mother in one person, this combination being regarded as a particularly terrifying and threatening one . . . At its period of maximal strength the child's sadism is centered round coitus between his parents. The death-wishes he feels against them during the primal scene or in his primal phantasies are associated with sadistic phantasies which are extraordinarily rich in content and which involve the sadistic destruction of his parents both singly and together. (Klein 1975, p. 132)

I do not know if that author was familiar with the Babylonian creation poem, but in her description of the paranoid-schizoid position of psychological development at the ontogenetic-individual level, one can find point-by-point parallels with the Babylonian myth, which describes psychological evolution at the phylogenetic-collective level. In psychology, just as in biology, ontogenesis recapitulates on a smaller scale (Heckel's law) phylopsychogenesis.

This "schizogenic" (Virel 1965) phase culminates in the separation of the primal syzygy (the combined parents): the differentiation of the maternal from the paternal principle. After this first sexual differentiation is generalized to the entire cosmos (earth and sky), which is created from original chaos (cosmogony, genesis), the creation of mankind (the anthropogony) follows:

"'Blood' will I form and cause bone to be; then will I set up a creature: 'Man' shall be his name! Yes, I will create Man!

Upon him shall the services of the gods be imposed that they may be at rest."[3]

But for that a divine sacrifice is required. Who is to be destroyed so that humanity can be born?

Kingu it was who created the strife, and caused Tiamat to revolt and prepare for battle. They bound him and held him before Ea; punishment they inflicted upon him by cutting the arteries of his blood. With his blood they created mankind. . . .[4]

From his blood, blended with the Earth Mother (Tiamat), was born poor humanity, who has never managed to make up for the original sin[5] of its unworthy first parents.

The Lunar Hero: Marduk's Passion or Anal-Genital Chiasma I

Marduk's passion demonstrates mythologically the integration of the paranoid-schizoid (solar) position into the depressive (lunar), and later manic (rebirth) positions (Briem 1951).

During the celebrations of the Babylonian new year, in the month of Nisan (March-April)—the future Easter—the ancients participated in an inversion-reversion of the cosmogonic and anthropogonic rhapsody or epic. Here it is no longer Marduk who destroys Kingu and then Tiamat, but inversely Kingu who, like the Egyptian Seth, puts Marduk to death. In this process there is a turning back against himself (a boomerang reversal) and an inversion-reversion of the sense of the sadistic, cannibalistic drives (*sense* in terms of both direction and meaning, as in the chiasma of figure 4). Marduk takes onto himself what he had previously made "other" or projected onto Apsu-Tiamat and Kingu. As subject, Marduk has to integrate the archetypal images of the primal syzygy (the combined parents): the monstrous mother (Tiamat), her animus (Apsu), and the monstrous double (Kingu). The only way for that integration to take place is for these archetypal images to turn against him and invert their sense. In understanding *sense* as direction, they turn from the other toward the subject; in the semantic understanding of *sense* as meaning, there is a realization that it is not the other who wants my destruction but, inversely, it is I myself who wants his destruction. One could actually die from this inversion-reversion, which belongs to any serious depression, whatever clinical form it might take. Initiation has always been therapeutic for this inversion-reversion of a drive: cruelty or initiatory mutilations of all orders, both moral and physical, constitute a lesser evil than total destruction. For example, genital castration is a lesser evil than *diasparagmos* and *omophagia*, both of which are oral.

It is from this very inversion-reversion that Marduk dies at the hands of Kingu, his monstrous double. All of Babylon then mourns and laments, saying, "Marduk is captive in the Mountain, who will rescue him?" The mountain means the Mother Mountain, her hollow and prominent breast, the Tartarus. The return to this breast is synonymous with the incest of the first birth (oral-anal in nature), and thus with death by *diasparagmos* and *omophagia*; in other words, it is death by the same kind of fragmentation that Marduk inflicted on Tiamat and Kingu so that genesis could be born from chaos. At this point genesis can only be formed from the fragments of the sacrificial son god. By way of this chiasmatic inversion-reversion, the agapes of cosmic and universal eros are born from wild, primitive orality.

The question "Who will rescue him?" is answered by Zarpanitu, a young and splendid virgin ("She of the silver reflections," thus lunar in nature). She is the lord's soul sister (anima); like Isis, she departs in search of her brother and lover with a heart full of tears. The son god has to sacrifice the mother of the first birth before the soul sister of the second birth can arise in him. And indeed Zarpanitu discovers in the shadow world the bloody and dismembered body of her lover. She puts him back together, reshapes him, nurses his wounds, nourishes him, and finally resurrects him on the third day of his nighttime passion.

During this part of the celebration, the believers divided into two camps, that of Marduk-Zarpanitu and that of Kingu-Tiamat, and reenacted the battle between the forces of good and evil. This mimetic drama was strewn with the wounded and even the dead. In an ancient age, the king—Marduk's representative on Earth—or a substitute (like the Greek *pharmakos*) was sacrificed. In later times, the high priest was content merely to tear off the insignias of the king's power, slap him, pull on his ears, and then hear his confession in public.

Following the lamenting and the violent battles during the passion came the joy of resurrection and the *hieros gamos* of the king—or of the priest—with the hierodule (sacred prostitute) in the city's ziggurat (Tower of Babel). Here, a manic defense followed the depressive position. The coming to pass of the phallus of rebirth and the uterus of the second birth is not as evident in Babylon as it was in Egypt, since the Babylonian myth was more archaic. But the *hieros gamos* did have the significance of a sacred union. In this union the two organs of procreation—procreation of the cosmos, life, and the anthropos—were deified, that is to say, they were de-animalized and then experienced in a suprachiasmatic consciousness.

Thus, with the exception of a few details, the passion of Marduk and Zarpanitu parallels that of Osiris and Isis. It explains phylopsychogenically, or at the collective level, what Klein has described as the "depressive position" at the ontopsychogenic or individual level. The passion is an inversion-reversion of the paranoid-schizoid position and integrates that position at a more evolved stage of the personality. Anality integrates orality, and genitality in turn integrates anality in the course of resurrection, cosmoanthropogony, and *hieros gamos*.

If we were to follow Freud's psychogenic schema, our own schema should come to a close after the oedipal stage at the age of six. The phallus of rebirth and the uterus of the second birth symbolize the archetypes of the genital father and mother—as opposed to the devouring and enslaving archetypal oral-anal father and mother (ogre and ogress). This opposition is all the more evident when we consider the fruit of the *hieros gamos*, the birth that takes place nine months later, which means near December 25. This divine child (*puer aeternus*) is called Nabu in Babylon and Horus (the Youth) in Egypt.[6] As the birth of the divine child falls at the winter solstice, this event symbolizes the inversion of day and night (a solar-lunar inversion) and the beginning of life's regeneration. This birth also symbolizes the new personality produced by the resurrection from the passion; and so it further symbolizes a new eros. Finally, the birth symbolizes a new logos (word). This image, however, remains a child, an adolescent, or a young adult. Along with him there is a corresponding young virgin-mother, called the Kore (such as Zapanitu, the redeemed Isis, and Mary), whose young animus he is, while she is for him a young mother-sister (anima). Nabu, Horus—even Jesus—will each take up the unfinished business left by the father (Marduk, Osiris, Jahweh), and, in the case of Babylon and Egypt, even avenge the father, in order to perpetuate the cycle of the family vendetta. This is a cycle of *ritualized* violence that by definition protects the collective from utter destruction. Consequently, the *puer aeternus* conceived in this postpassion *hieros gamos* clearly tells us that in these myths we are still dealing with childhood psychogenesis.

The young virgin-mother is definitely a Kore, a *puella.* She is the one that Freud describes as entertaining the "fantasy of having a child by the father"—beyond the usual sense of castration, where the child by the father takes the place of the missing penis. My idea of the daughter's castration does not agree with Freud's. The girl is not castrated of a penis but of her toothed uterus or vagina (Montrelay 1977). Nevertheless, the fantasy of having a child by the father is certainly there, beyond our own vision of a girl's castration. She desires, then, a child of the phallus of rebirth, as opposed to the dismembering and perforating penis of the primal Father, the animus of the Mother. She desires it in her uterus of second birth. We see here again that mother and father are nothing but the correlates (O′ image-objects) from the actualization of the O image-objects, which spring from psychic archetypal/instinctual reality.

Consequently, the phallus of rebirth and the uterus of the second birth are still, at this psychogenetic stage, the archetypal representatives, of Father and Mother, which are experienced in "otherness" in the concrete mother-father relationship. Once Osiris is reborn and Isis redeemed, just as when Marduk is reborn and Zarpanitu redeemed, each couple again becomes *puer* and *puella.*

Passage from Genital I to Genital II

This passage is one that mirrors Freud's phases of latency and puberty, and once again it evokes the myth of Isis and Osiris.

Not until puberty do the phallus and uterus of rebirth relate to physical and concrete objects other than mother and father, which can authentically be designated by the terms *animus* and *anima*. In time, the man (or men) or the woman (or women) in one's life realizes these archetypal images, which resulted from our first passions. We experience new passions, good or bad, always both. Each of them is an attempt at rebirth, at times successful and at times not. As we experience diverse passions, we await the coming of the second half of life, which takes place at about thirty-six years of age, assuming an average life span of seventy-two years. The cycles seem to last twelve years. (An astrologer might find this an appropriate number for those under the sign of Jupiter.)

These three steps can be summarized in a new, simplified pyramidal schema. In this diagram, the configuration of O and O′ image-objects is omitted at each level.

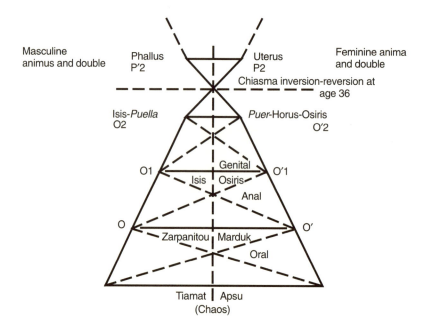

Figure 5

From the Genital II Chiasma to the Anticipation of Death in the Here and Now

The Love Object Becomes Subject

From about thirty-six to forty-eight years of age (obviously exact ages may vary), we live out a new passion, one quite similar to that of our two son gods Osiris and Marduk: we have to become conscious of our love object. We realize that this object, which we have already more or less "incorporated," to the point of fusing with it and considering it merely as an enslaved appendage of our own being, is in fact also a subject. We come to the realization that this subject is like us, and that we must consider its dignity equal to our own and love it as it is, rather than as we would wish it to be. In a word, we must change the possessiveness of the eros instinct, which lies below the chiasma, into a giving spiritual eros, depicted as lying above the chiasma. We become aware that the phallus or uterus of rebirth, which up to now we had seen as other in the man or woman in our life, in fact belongs to us. The woman has to integrate the animus, and the man the anima: each has to integrate cannibalism, slavishness, and possessiveness, which at this point still reign in them. As this is achieved, the subjects, Isis and Osiris, which correspond respectively to anima and animus (horizontally: O-Oα and vertically: O-P'α for example, see figure 4), can be metamorphosized at the same time.

The chiasma that this new step produces is by definition central, as it relates to midlife. The chiasma reproduces exactly the steps already familiar to us from the Marduk and Osiris myths, but at a higher level—or spiral—of ontopsychogenesis. The same archetypal images appear at this level, but they take on a new meaning. The suffering theme remains the same, and the task is still to invert-revert the instinctual flow. Withdrawing libido from an external, physical, and concrete object, on which it has already been cast, is felt by the primitive as a loss of soul and by the child as emptiness, dismemberment, depression, death. One has lost one's soul, which has been confused with the external object. Thus, to lose one's soul is at the same time to lose this object. The loss is twofold, encompassing both substance and psychic energy coming from the other, who up until now had served as a psychological support. The stronger the fusion with the other, and the greater the dependence on him or her (there is no stronger dependence than the one known to exist in sado-masochistic fusion), the stronger the feelings of loss, emptiness, nothingness, and death, until our eventual concrete death.

This fusional love is pregenital love par excellence: it is at once oral because it incorporates, and anal because it enslaves.[7] Genital possessiveness is its last offshoot, plunging its roots into earlier strata that taint it with their characteristics. That is why castration, as obviously genital as it is, at the same time always refers back more or less to the anal and oral drives. There is no genital castration that does not refer back to diasparagmic and omophagic cannibalism and to master-slave slavishness—the lunar myths of Osiris and Marduk have clearly shown us that. And if we were to refer to the self-castration of Attis, we would have yet more evidence that the self-castrating gesture of that Phrygian son god was used as a way to avoid as radically as possible a regression to the instinctual pregenital hell, or death by dismemberment (*diasparagmos*) or fragmentation.

Yet, it is this very regression that we must experience symbolically and as initiation during the second half of life. First, we regress to the "genital belly" of the symbolic mother of the second birth. This regression occurs when we are about thirty-six to forty-eight years of age. As described above, this step is crucial *because it is at this stage that we become conscious of our psychospiritual sex double and of our psychospiritual sex complement (animus/anima)*. It is no longer the woman in our life who is charged with incarnating for us the Eternal Woman (Isis, Zarpanitu, and indeed Eve) and making present and having realized within us the Eternal Man (Osiris, Marduk, and indeed Adam), which is the internal object of her own desire. Now it is we ourselves who must be conscious that the Eternal Woman is the internal object ($O2\alpha$ in figure 6, below) of our own heterosexual desire (anima), while the Eternal Man is the internal object ($O2$) of our own homosexual desire (double).[8] Anima (complement) and double should no longer be confused, neither with the physical, concrete woman of one's life, nor with the double that she embodies for us and who is her own complement (animus), nor, finally, with one's own sex drive, which is physical and thus symbolically castrated.

That is why, at this suprachiasmic stage, the letters used to designate different positions must be changed. The psychospiritual doubles and complements, which are differentiated and individuated from the instinctual and physical objects, we will designate with the letter *P*. *P* is for *palingenic*, since it is from the moment of these suprachiasmic (psychospiritual) engrams that we can safely (i.e., symbolically) confront the necessary regressions to instinctual stages. These regressions are necessary in order to purge, or redeem, that which still binds us through fusion, imagination, and maya to genital objects and concurrently, as we saw earlier, to pregenital objects. We are confronting once more the genital, anal, and oral levels of the underworld, but from then on we are anchored to the underworlds associated with the suprachiasmic second birth (heavens). Palingenesis is the return to life following a real or apparent death—that is, it means having to die in order to become. Each descent into the instinctual underworld is, in fact, a new passion. The *imaginal* image-objects (P) are opposed to the *imaginary* image-objects (O)—even though they are identical—because they are differentiated and above all individuated: they are no longer involved in the fusion/confusion of subject with object, or I with Other. The "little other" (Lacan's "o") has become the "big Other," but at the same time the "little subject" has become the "big Subject."

Through this process Madame Isis (my concrete wife or lover) has become for me an Other, an authentic alter ego. I respect her freedom to be for herself who she really is within herself (see figure 6, below), and if I love her, it is for what she is and not for what I want her to be or what I believe she is in an imaginary way. Her instinctual representation in me ($O2\alpha$, the imaginary instinctual anima) henceforth connects with a spiritual representation of her, now engrammed as $P2\alpha$ (the imaginal, individuated anima). The vertical conjunction $O2\alpha$-$P2\alpha$ effects the inversion-reversion from instinctual to spiritual and back (from need, to desire and love, to eros). The representation P2 has become a rather irrational linking "organ" between my inner life and the outer world. It is my feminine soul, which is now recognized and individuated; it is my metaphorical function, my sensitive and intuitive (irrational) dialogue with the world (Jung 1921), and connects horizontally with eros-logos. Eros-logos, in turn, is a result of the inversion-reversion of the

43

shadow of my instinctual anima (O′2α), which is allegorized in the myth of Madame Hathor (the famous "step-mother"). Above the chiasma Madame Hathor becomes, along with eros-logos, the *spiritus rector*, or spirit guide, of loving and mystical discourse. (She is the future Sophia and celestial Mother, who is here still reduced to Aphrodite.)

Mister Isis (my instinctual, physical, and concrete penis) engrammed in O2 (my ego) and freed from the imaginary fusion with the animus of Madame Isis (which used to constitute her specular, imaginary, instinctual double), now connects with her new suprachiasmic engram in P2, the foundation for the double that is spiritual, imaginal, individuated but no longer specular. The vertical conjunction O2-P2 effects the inversion-reversion between the instinctual and the spiritual (need-desire and love-eros). The representation P2 has become a more rational linking "organ" between my inner world and the outer world. P2 is my acknowledged, individuated, masculine soul, my dialogue of feeling and thought (rational thought) with the world (Jung 1921), in horizontal conjunction with logos-eros (P′2). Logos-eros, in turn, is the result of the inversion-reversion of the shadow of my instinctual double (O′2), which we have seen allegorized in myth by Mister Seth and which is the core of my persecutory (paranoid) homosexuality. Above the chiasma, Mister Seth becomes, along with the logos-eros, the *spiritus rector* (spirit guide) for the discourse of law in its juridicial, scientific, and spiritual aspects (the future Christos and celestial Father, which here is still reduced to eros).[9]

It is these *imaginal* doubles and spiritual complements (eros-logos and logos-eros), which, once anchored (engrammed, encoded), allow us to descend into instinct (passion) facing no more danger than a deep-sea diver who is linked to the surface by his boat full of equipment.

At right is a rough sketch of this new chiasma, superimposed over the outline of figure 4.

Caritas

From about forty-eight to sixty years of age, the individual who has been "called" has to go beyond love for one's intimates and pass over to a love for one's neighbor (caritas). Already that is a

The Babylonian Myth of Marduk and Tiamat

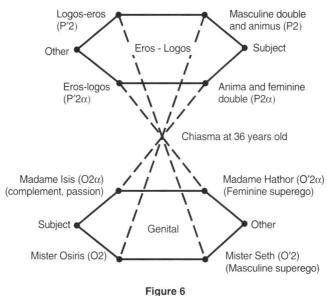

Figure 6

"Crisscrossing pyramids," here seen in its application to the masculine psyche. To apply this schema to a woman's psyche, replace Osiris with Isis, Seth with Hathor, and so forth.

very rare step for anyone to take. At present, Mother Teresa—winner of the 1979 Nobel Peace Prize—offers us a rather striking example of it. Indeed, she lives among the vermin and among those dying of the plague, that is to say, she lives within the full "anality" of a country that has not, collectively, economically and politically, surpassed that slavish, anal stage. Yet, she transcends the slavishness of putrescence—for herself and for the few whom she helps in their living and dying—through her love for the people around her. In fact, the passage from genital eros-logos to caritas is made on the one hand by the integration (differentiation and individuation) of anal libido that cathects the genital drive (the first phase, which we have just seen). On the other hand, there must also be an integration of true anal libido, still lived in a way, but in a sadistic homosexual way (which the myth of Osiris and Seth describes to us) or in any case, through our propensity to submit the Other to our own will to power.[10]

Even an apparently altruistic and self-sacrificing attitude

45

contains, deep down, this same concern with making the Other submit. We must be wary of that serpent (Apopis-Seth) which is coiled up within any "good deed" when we try to follow the example of Mother Teresa by practicing charity. The road to hell is paved with good intentions, even good intentions that have been acted out. In order for Mother Teresa's actions to be authentically charitable—that is, canonically charitable, to the point of holiness—one must be convinced that she has no need for the objects of her charity in order to satiate this slavish will to power. In her case it is entirely possible, but not certain. That is what I would ask for if I were—God forbid—the devil's advocate at her eventual canonization proceedings. In any case, her actions have amply earned her the Nobel Prize.

This example shows us the extreme rarity of such an undertaking which, on our schema, joins together the image-objects [(O1-O'1)-(O1α-O'1α)]- [(P'1α-P1α) - (P'1-P1)], in a new bi-quaternity pyramid that we add to figure 6 to form a new schema:

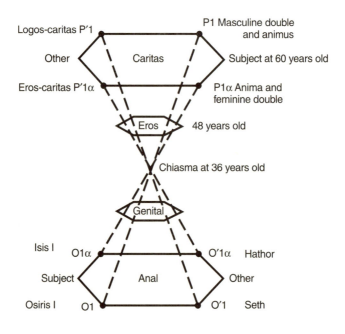

Figure 7

An extension of figure 6, including the instinctual anal stage and its spiritual complement, caritas, discussed below.

46

For this new phase, we return to the anal level (Duat) of figure 4 and, by inversion-reversion centered on the chiasma at thirty-six years of age, we effect the conjunctions that take place at the caritas level. The conjunctions are as follows: Osiris I (01) unites with the individuation of his double (P1), which is also the complement (animus) of Isis; Isis I (O1α) unites with the individuation of her double (P1α), which is also the complement (anima) of Osiris; Seth (O′1) connects with the individuation of the masculine *spiritus rector* (commonly called the celestial Father) which we call here logos-caritas (P′1); and Hathor (O′1α) connects with the individuation of the feminine *spiritus rector* (commonly called the celestial Mother) which we call here eros-caritas (P′1α). Between these two strata lie the genital-eros conjunctions developed earlier. Necessarily, the anal-genital conjunctions as well as the eros-caritas (and the genital-eros) ones continue to function. In this way, we can effect the individuation of the de-pressive—and manic—core of the corresponding Kleinian position. The first anal-genital conjunctions—from about three to six years of age—do not constitute, properly speaking, an individuation, but rather a *differentiation*, in relation to the *concrete* mother and father objects found on the side of the O′ objects, that is to say, on the side of the Other. Individuation is a form of differentiation, but a differentiation that takes place in relation to the archetypal (and instinctual) objects found on the side of the O objects, or on the side of the Subject. Of course the O and O′ objects are individualized concurrently, but in the first case the differentiation is imposed by the concrete object (Other), while in the second case the individuation is self-imposed by the Subject (who should not be confused with the Self).

Agape

From sixty to seventy-two years of age, the individual who has been called has to expand this love of neighbor (caritas) even more, into universal love (agape). If caritas is extremely rare, agape is even more so. In the fifteenth century, it is said that there was a priest who lived for twenty years on unleavened bread, the consecrated host, for his only food. He was called Niklaus von der Flue (Nicholas of Flue). Pius XII canonized him in 1947, and he is the patron saint of the Swiss. He, in turn, was putting into practice the myth of the Fisher King as recounted in the Grail legend (Chrétien de Troyes 1982). It is said that the Fisher King lived on the Eucharist alone for twelve years, until Perceval delivered him from his tortures. A maiden brought the Eucharist to him at each meal in the famous vase (chalice) known as the Grail. A valet carried next to the Grail the lance with the blood of the Savior.

We have said that the long-enduring ritual of cannibalism was lost in the Paleolithic twilight, but its apotheosis bursts out in the Christic myth of Jesus of Nazareth, particularly in the famous Last Supper. There, on the eve of his personal sacrifice, he gives to his apostles, who are gathered around the table, bread and wine, which are said to be his body and his blood (mystical agapes). Each day Catholic priests still perform this transubstantiation of bread and wine into the body and blood of the Sacrificed One. It is from this body and this blood that the priest spiritually nourishes himself and his flock.

The Fisher King of the Grail, like the monk from Flue, also took his bodily nourishment from the host. The facts apply quite precisely to the Swiss saint. It is appropriate, then, to speak of a mystical paraphysiology that lends support to an equally mystical parapsychology. "Somation," as discussed above—the mutation of the genes of neocortical cells (soma, as opposed to germen) that occurs by means of the passion-laden sacrifice of wild cannibalism (or, as above, of wild slavishness and possessiveness)—is here as good a hypothesis as any other, and one with the advantage of telling us something about this paraphysiology, which up until now was beyond our means of investigation.

If the phenomenon of somation is extremely rare to the degree that it has been taken by Nicholas of Flue—and probably by many other anorexics who are unknown or who have been written up in studies of pathology[11]—it is much less rare at the level of many food-related asceticisms, particularly vegetarianism. Somation is even more common at the level of the primary neocortical engrams of P image-objects, which are induced by the first training and ritualization of the oral drive. The fact that a child breastfeeds every three hours is already an example of a prohibition against cannibalism, and a transgression within the law of this same prohibition. This original ritualization already causes a "sacrificial" metamorphosis from cannibalism into agape.

The final period, lasting from sixty to seventy-two years of age, brings to completion this metamorphosis of the lower levels of the psyche into a conscious and self-willing paranoid-schizoid transcendence. Two more levels can now be added to our schema, the oral and agape levels, with their two quaternities: $[(O\text{-}O') -(O\alpha\text{-}O'\alpha)] - [(P'\alpha\text{-}P\alpha) -(P'\text{-}P)]$.

At this final stage of development our eschatalogical Sophia-Christos syzygy is inscribed. All the lunar son and lover gods having to do with suffering (Tammuz, Dumuzi, Marduk, Osiris, Adonis . . . Jesus) are "Christoi," that is, consecrated by being anointed. They are anointed by being reborn in Sophia.

For this final image, we will turn not to *Proverbs*, nor to the *Book of Wisdom*; rather, we will ask Antoine de Saint-Exupéry to describe Sophia as she appeared to him when he was lost in the middle of the Egyptian desert after his plane crash in 1936—when he was broken, exhausted, thirsty, and awaiting his imminent death:

> It is not at all by the randomness of childhood language that the image of love touched me with as much force as the image of death [. . .]. When I was bedded down in the earth, during my last thirsty hours in Egypt, that great calm virgin sat beside me. She had quenched my thirst, she had poured serenity over me with the milk of the stars. I was filled with an incomprehensible and limitless happiness, and I didn't believe I would make it until morning [. . .]. In the last hours, she spread over me a huge velvet cape.[12]

Sophia is mother of life, mother of death, mother of rebirth, "the spirit which animates all men" (*Book of Wisdom* 1:6), "friend of humanity" (7:23), "laborer of all things (7:21), "who inhabits an intelligent and saintly spirit" (7:22), "reflection of the eternal light, flawless mirror" (7:26), "conductor of souls, she leads toward God and assures immortality" (6:18 and 8:13). Celestial Sophia, offspring of the lunar Zarpanitu and the infernal Tiamat and emerging on the universal eros (eros-agape); celestial Christos, offspring of the lunar Marduk and the infernal Apsu-Kingu and emerging on the universal word (logos-agape);

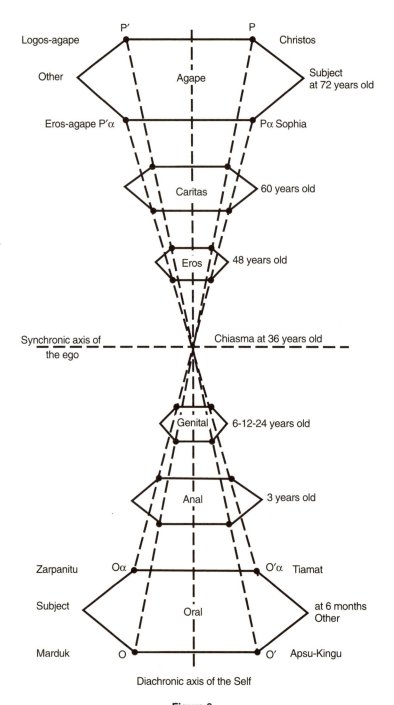

Figure 8

"Crisscrossing pyramids," consisting of all psychogenic stages. The oral level corresponds to the Babylonian mythological stage, while the anal and genital aspects correspond to the two Egyptian stages.

Sophia, archetypal representation of the cosmic eros; Christos, archetypal representation of the cosmic logos.

These last conjunctions are otherwise designated by *pneuma, nous, atman, self, other*[13] (absolute Selfness, absolute Otherness). They connote the most universal degree of religiousness (from Latin *religere*, "to bind together"). Although those who attain this conjunction are rare, we all can have at least a vague intuition of it—sense a vague foreknowledge, experience a vague presence—because we all have at least an embryo of the engrams of the image-objects P-P′, Pα-P′α.

Notes

1. Esharra is a poetic name for the earth, according to A. Heidel. See *The Babylonian Genesis* (1951), p. 43, note 96. (translator's note)

2. Solié cites these scattered passages from tablets 4 and 5 of the *Enuma Elish*, quoted here from *The Babylonian Genesis* (1951), pp. 39-44. (translator's note)

3. *The Babylonian Genesis* (1951), p. 46, tablet 6, verses 5-8. (translator's note)

4. Ibid., p. 47, tablet 6, verses 29-33. (translator's note)

5. The eating of "forbidden fruit" is clearly indicated here in the children's devouring. The Genesis of the Hebrews is a product of the Babylonian Genesis, among others.

6. Mithras and Jesus Christ were also born at the same time of the year.

7. But it is also the one which will produce the eros-caritas and eros-agape, as we will see.

8. The process is inverted for a woman.

9. A parallel argument can be made concerning a woman's psyche, as her animus is linked to logos-eros and her double to eros-logos.

10. The Jungian antithesis to eros, but which flirts particularly with thanatos.

11. A sixty-three-year-old woman was brought to Paris from the countryside by her father to consult with me. The father, at eighty-five, was much healthier than his daughter. They had both come to ask me if it was necessary to continue feeding this poor woman intravenously; for fifteen years she had been hospitalized every month for anorexia that dated to her adolescence but that had gotten worse fifteen years before she consulted me. Her aggravated condition necessitated these monthly hospitalizations and caused her to go back to the convent

where she had found shelter when she was twenty. Obviously, a number of drug therapies had already been attempted. I advised them to refuse the next hospitalization. Comforted, she began eating a few vegetables and fruits. When I saw her next, a month later, she had gained three kilos. The doctor who had sent her to me did not have her hospitalized as usual. Three months went by this way, and one day the father and my colleague telephoned me: she had fallen back into her anorexia. I asked to see her again. At this last meeting, she expressly asked me for permission to "leave this valley of misery," having, according to her, sufficiently fought against death to have earned the right to die without having to feel that she was a failure. Three weeks later, her father and her doctor told me that she had died in the greatest possible peace.

12. From an unpublished letter of 1936, from M. Quesnel, notes and documents, in Chevrier (1959).

13. See Solié (1980a) for definitions of the universal Self (Great Self) and the universal Other (Great Other).

5

Laura's Return

When we left her earlier, Laura had not yet undergone the last change that would be required of her—she remained in the anal underworld of Osiris-Seth and Isis as well as in the oral one of Marduk-Kingu and Tiamat. She stayed trapped between the paranoid-schizoid position and the depressive position.

As noted, she described herself as "empty," just like the space around her: she felt unstructured and was plagued by terrifying monsters. This imaginary space, which was quasi-hallucinatory and seriously phobic, therefore compelled her to seek the concrete presence of the other, on whom she had conferred the counterphobic capacity of reassuring permanence. This need explains the massive transferences that my Freudian colleagues had gently dismissed. Laura said that she would forever need to be "supported by her surroundings." In this statement we come close to the "devouring" transferences of the psychotic, who only feels capable of going on by relying on the presence of the concrete object. He or she fails to disentangle objective psychic reality (which produces the O image-objects) from objective physical reality (which produces the O′ image-objects) and has lost the ability to symbolize or to rely upon the imaginal O-O′ (or Oα-O′α). Besides the concrete object which she had empowered in this way, only meetings with her mother in the beyond of the afterlife allowed her to exorcize the therioanthropomorphic images of death, which are analogous to those of Egyptian or

Hindu mythology. She said of her mother, "Her presence gives me security, consoles me and heals me." The mother of life fought against the mother of death, Zarpanitu was in combat with Tiamat, and Isis exorcised Hathor.

This need for a champion explains Laura's long reveries in the presence of her mother's photographs and her mother's favorite possessions, as well as her habit of listening to her mother's voice as recorded on cassettes at a family gathering a few days before her death. All of these things Laura shared with me, even leaving some at my house for safekeeping. At this point she wanted me to go with her and become acquainted with the apartment she used to share with her mother—this apartment was near where I had lived during the same period. With difficulty, I dissuaded her, and instead we reconstructed this heavily cathected place by drawing floor plans, leaving no nook or cranny undescribed. Her older brother even came to my office to confirm the exact details of these diagrams. Laura contemplated them for a long time afterward, mentally going over them in every direction, reliving the memories attached to each spot. While she did that, we often listened to her mother's recorded voice and looked at her photograph: "You become Mama," she used to say to me, "thus I can fuse in such a way that I can maintain, paradoxically, some distance, since I externalize mother onto you, thereby freeing myself from her." This sentence, spoken at the end of a year of psychotherapy, exemplifies the reversible nature of "possession" by the dead woman and the "depossession" of Laura. A shaman would have interpreted this intense link as a "theft of the soul" by the spirit of the deceased and, in a trance, his double would have departed for the realm of the shadows. The shaman would face the perils of that journey, as well as engage in a dangerous combat with the soul-stealing spirit of the deceased, to retrieve the soul of his patient, only to face once again the same perils on the way back. All this to reincorporate the recovered—and redeemed—soul into the "empty" body of the patient, which would thereafter be "filled."

This operation reflects one that Egyptian priests performed on the mummified bodies of their "patients" (or "initiates") in the ceremony called the "opening of the mouth and eyes"—and of all the other senses. Through this sacrament, the word—and the sense of taste—was restored to the mouth, images to the eyes, sounds to the ears, smells to the nose, the sense of tactility to touch. In short, the dead were reanimated; the soul reintegrated its revitalizing functions. That is what Laura and I did during this phase of reincorporating the dead mother, who was taken to be the mother of life. Her Isisian soul was reinfused within her, reanimating her. By transferring onto me this mother of life, Laura objectified it—distanced herself from it, as she said—but, at the same time, she distanced herself from the vampirelike Hathorian or Tiamatian mother of death.

Laura frequently had homosexual dreams or fantasies. As a child, she had fantasized for a long time about becoming her mother's husband—basically, she had an inverted oedipal complex. She used to pull on her clitoris, trying to become a boy. This shows the extent to which her psychological sex complement (animus) possessed her, in the sense of a shamanic, theological, and psychiatric possession.[1] One might think that when she lost this love object (her mother/wife), she would be losing her psychological sex double (Egyptian *ka*) at the same time. From then on, her masculine complement (Egyptian *ba-ib*) would have to submit to the Osirian ordeals of death, dismemberment, and castration[2] by the infernal shadow of this complement (Seth, in the myth). In concrete reality the shadow became confused, not with the father, about whom the mother cared very little, but with her mother's own masculine sex complement (animus), which manifested itself clearly in her—to the point that Laura felt a part of her mother's death. There we find once more the original syzygy of Babylon, Tiamat-Apsu (the fantasy of the "combined parents"), as well as the paranoid-schizoid orality that goes with it and with the diasparagmic (dismembering) Seth of Egyptian myth.

Laura's depersonalization ("loss of soul") was such that, if she had some trouble affectively recognizing her mother in a photograph, she had difficulty even recognizing her own reflection in a mirror. Therefore, during the time she refamiliarized herself with her mother, we also spent long sessions contemplating her reflection in the mirror. I had to look in the mirror with her, and her own recognition of herself became possible by my recognition of her. Our two sets of eyes converged on her image and conferred beauty on it. In the framework of this "opening of the eyes" (scopic drives, as in the Eye of Horus and of Ra), it occurred to her to ask me to gaze on and acknowledge her nude body in a similar way. Just as with the idea of going back to her childhood apartment, actually acting out this exhibitionism was appropriately avoided. Instead, we read together her childhood and adolescent papers, her letters, her diary, and so forth. We did this because the "primary" and "grandiose" Self (Kohut 1974, Neumann 1976), which emerges from being recognized in the mirror by the Other, demands an "opening of all the senses," all the "inter-sensoria," "inter-sensitivities," and "inter-motricities." The "jubilatory assumption" (according to Lacan) that follows this recognition signals the birth, not of the ego, but of the "grandiose Self" (according to Kohut), which is very close to primary narcissism.[3] In the course of this new birth, the manic position appears to consciousness as an epiphany, complementing, by means of compensation, the depressive position of the dismembered and castrated Osiris.

The "grandiose Self" is the reborn Osiris (see figure 4), as is any deceased person (or initiate) being reborn in Osiris. Its rebirth takes place at the end of its journey through the shadowy Duat (the alchemists' *nigredo*), in which it confronts the guardians of the Pylons (thresholds), who are armed with knives, as well as the chthonian monsters (underground, infernal beings) sheltered and nourished by any Inferno worthy of the name as well as by any alchemy characterized by sadomasochistic, cannibalistic, and enslaving instincts.

In ancient times, mummification was as a rule preceded by *diasparagmos*. "Untouchable" specialists, segregated in villages near the necropoles, dismembered the corpses of the deceased, tore their flesh into pieces, disemboweled them, and embalmed them (anointed them). After this, the pieces were reassembled (re-membered): the whole body was reconstituted and embalmed (anointed) piece by piece, but now shrunken and gathered together to reflect an embryonic state so that it might go through a second gestation before rebirth. The old shamanistic ritual of *diasparagmos* was thereby perpetuated, and both Seth's dismembering gesture and Isis's unifying one were renewed. Later mummification techniques left out this archaic ritual of dismemberment, but obvious outlines of it continued to appear, symbolically, within the embalming process of mummification.

Let us reiterate that mummification was meant to conserve

the earthly body so that the double (*ka*) and the shadow (*khaibit*) did not die before the soul (*ba*) and the heart (*ib*) could be born to the deceased in Duat, so that the body of resurrection (*iakhu*), the spirit (*sahu*) and the new name (*ren*) might come into being. In the same way, the initiates (anticipating the ritual of death in the here and now) submitted to the initiation process in an empty and solemn crypt of the temple—the tomb—where, hypnotized by priests, they regressed and were led to experience this "loss of soul" and of their double. The hypnosis opened them to terrifying images of the shadow, which they were forced to confront in an effort to metamorphosize them or in any case to overcome them. This process is like that of Marduk fighting Tiamat's monsters, and the monster Tiamat herself, so that cosmos and anthropos could be born from her remains.

In the same way, Laura spontaneously lay down on the couch and covered herself, piece by piece, with all the cushions she could find. There, for more than six months, she joined her mother in Duat and with her confronted the serpent Apopis (Seth), guardian of the underworld of eternal damnation who "multiplies the fire and projects it with violence." There, she evolved between the "scales of the monster."

She journeyed through the glacial spaces of the regions of Urnes and of the dead and dismembered Osiris. She met the sun, Ra,[4] with the head of a ram, who had come from the west. He had left his daytime barge for the one he rides at night and was fighting there, like Laura, against the forces of destruction and death that came from the caverns of Sokaris (in antiquity the god of the dead of Memphis), where the darkness of the underworld is like the abysmal waters at the bottom of the sea. There, the night barge of the sun was transformed before her eyes into a long, invisible serpent.

At the sixth Pylon (portal), she saw thousands of souls in the form of birds (*ba*), and strange goddesses carrying in their hands the Eye of Horus. She also saw the golden scarab, the sun as Khepri, ready for his rebirth in the Orient. But Apopis avidly tried to drink the water which carried his barge, filling the seventh circle of Duat with viscous and poisonous spirals. She also saw the enemies of Osiris, partisans of Apopis-Seth, beheaded by lionheaded demons and bound forever in the infernal Duat. She crossed the water and the fire of the underground world

(Agarit) and then saw the rowers abandon the solar barge, as the towing line became a serpent. Finally, she witnessed the rebirth of the new sun, between the thighs of the celestial goddess Nut, mother of the fourfold representations of Osiris, Seth, Isis, and Nephtis. She saw Osiris welcome the revived sun and place him upon his celestial orbit. Then the dead rejoiced, while the living arose to contemplate the power and light of the new god, born of himself after his nocturnal metamorphoses and trials. Khepri, Ra, and Atoum were reborn from the nocturnal Osiris. Let us put into a schema this cycle, with the elements day-night, solar-lunar, and conscious-unconscious, typical of the solar and lunar heroes.

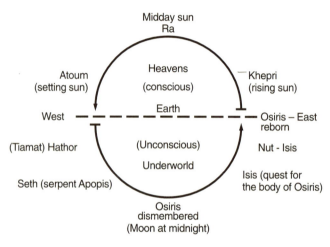

Figure 9

The twelve hours of the Osirian darkness (the twelve Pylons) lasted six months for Laura, thus about fifteen days for each portal. Beyond that point (but also in a certain rhythm, because our sessions occurred three times a week), she began to restructure her *personal* historical time-space. Thus she spent the first six months structuring the *collective* historical time-space: that of ancient Egypt, in this case, which meant a history dating back five thousand years.

C. G. Jung calls this collective historical overview the "collective unconscious" to distinguish it clearly from individual history, which he calls the "personal unconscious" (familial, much like that of Freud). This distinction was made because, as we have seen, just as ontogenesis in a briefer and simpler form recapitulates phylogenesis, ontopsychogenesis in the same way recapitulates phylopsychogenesis. In order for Laura's ontopsychogenesis to be constructed—or reconstructed—it demanded that she turn to the portion of the phylopsychogenesis of the human Imaginary relevant to her own psychological structure and its inherent problem (that of the mother's daughter and lover) (Solié 1980b).

Having become her mother in the transference, I was thus by turns Tiamat-Hathor, the devourers, and Zarpanitu-Isis, the helpful mothers and sisters of the second life. But I was also, as we have seen, the animus of these mothers, sometimes solar, violent (violating), and perforating, sometimes lunar, violated, dismembered, castrated—and finally reborn. Laura was all these things by turn, right along with me—or else she was the object of these phenomena.[5] In short, each archetype of the collective (phylopsychogenetic) history was incarnated in her and in me, creating a personal (ontopsychogenetic) history, as she should have been able to do during her childhood and adolescent years. During those early years, her parents could have concretely revealed this objective psychic reality to her, as light reveals vision to the eye.

It was after this work of imprinting ("incarnating") the O-O′ and Oα-O′α objects at their different synchronic levels (oral, anal, and genital) that one day, just before my vacation, she asked me where I would be going. I said the name of the village where I had grown up, and right away she told me that her family name had been the name of my village until the seventeenth century, when her father's family had left it to go north. Was she making this up? She answered my unspoken question the next day by bringing me genealogical proof, which I was then easily able to verify. This link was a striking coincidence, and in fact especially so when added to the fact that she had come to me at the very moment that I had become engrossed in a study of the Great Mother goddess.[6] Add to that another coincidence, namely, that the apartment where she grew up (and which we had so painstakingly reconstructed together) was near the apartment where I had lived during the same time. Only one psychotherapist in Paris (within France, within Europe, or anywhere else) could have met all these requirements, and "by accident" she stumbled across that person. There is neither time nor space here to mull over these bizarre phenomena.[7] Several months later, when it was once again time for a vacation, she asked permission to visit me in this place of her original paternal lineage. There we went all through the region, which she undoubtedly would never have visited without this opportunity, and most importantly we found her ancestral lands (also included in her name) just a few kilometers from my village.

And so to the collective and individual histories was now added the history of her own lineage, which made a bridge between the first two and was in turn integrated into her general psychic economy.

Her chaos little by little was changed into cosmos, genesis, and history, both sacred and profane.

Notes

1. Freud's concept of penis envy, here amplified within Jung's concept of animus.

2. Here we are not making much of the guilt attached to these incestuous homosexual fantasies and dreams, but let us note it in passing. During treatment, Laura had sex with several men. Clitoral self-stimulation was evidently predominant.

3. In which the part drives and their objects are unified in a more or less total gestalt (structure, form).

4. Khepri at the rising sun, Ra at noon, Atoum at the setting sun, Osiris for the night.

5. But she was above all the dead and mutilated Osiris, her complement-animus; and I was for her Isis, my complement-anima, in whom she rebirthed herself just as Osiris rebirths the dead and his initiates. Obviously, six months could in no way exhaust the palingenesic work of this phylopsychogenic matrix.

6. Jung called such phenomena synchronicity.

7. See *Cahiers de psychologie jungienne*, December 1980 (1, place de l'Ecole Militaire, 75007 Paris).

Part Two

Mythanalysis Applied

6

Nocturnal Dreaming: Manifestation of Objective Psychic Reality and Witness to Its Transformation

Laura's case, which provided a model for our mythanalytic methodology, demonstrates a rather varied treatment. Such treatment is dictated by patients' dreamlike (daytime) fantasies, and it ranges from having therapists simply listen in silence to having them participate most actively in the therapy. Laura's nocturnal dreams, though numerous and consequently active in her psyche, were actually used very little. To show a complementary treatment approach, here are two short vignettes from other cases in which nocturnal dreams emerge as the driving force for progress in treatment.

Leda

Leda, a twenty-four-year-old student, gives us a good example of the movement that occurs in dreams from the ophidian (serpentine) phallus of the Great Mother—her animus—toward the phallus of the Father, and finally to the patient's own animus complement (through psychological integration or engramming of Seth/Osiris or of Apsu/Kingu and Marduk).

This young woman, who had a hysterical-bulimic psychic structure, came to see me after experiencing an episode of "bodily transformation," in which she felt that her head had been separated from her body.[1] This state was accompanied by a feeling of suffocation, a flight of ideas, and suicidal ideation. During this episode full of psychic eclipses of consciousness, an emaciated man forced himself upon her in a "numinous" way. He was at once fascinating and terrifying, divine and demonic: spiritual and instinctual, imaginal and imaginary.

Leda compared the "apparition" of this man to the apparitions of serpents in her dreams that had evoked the same impressions in her since she was eight years old. At that age, she dreamed that her room was a birdcage whose bars were enormous, long boa constrictors, who paralyzed her with panic. One or two of these boas actually wrapped themselves around the bed, "binding" her to it. To this dream we could add one more about a dog who bit her at the base of her spinal column.

A little later, she had another recurring dream: of a rope/serpent that crossed an infinite black space, and a dark man who appeared, a menacing man who was tied to this luminous yellow rope. He could become extraordinarily huge or extraordinarily tiny. She could touch neither the cord nor the man; they always escaped her. She ended up holding only emptiness.

Just before Leda came to me, while she was still in psychotherapy with a female psychologist, she dreamed that she was climbing the stairs of this psychologist's building and that, when she came to the fourth floor, her way was blocked by a snake curled around the bars of the railing. In order to reach her therapist, she would have to accept being at least "touched" by the snake.

Another dream involved a serpent/crocodile who chased her down an endless hallway: she tried to trap it in a huge clear plastic bag, but it fought back, "piercing through" the bag, and blood flooded the ground.

In a very recent dream, she was in her grandmother's garden. Her parents were there. From a pear tree in the middle, a serpent came down and "ran" extremely fast toward her mother, who ran away. Then it turned toward Leda. It had the head of a beaver. She jumped but the serpent/beaver managed to "sting" her. And while she ran toward her mother, screaming, the animal calmly stayed with her father.

And finally, the last one that we will relate here (because there are many more like these): Leda found herself in a room with no windows, artificially lit. On the table there was a vase, out of which a very beautiful and very thin serpent rose up. It wanted to be with her, it chased her. She took refuge in the kitchen, with her parents. Her father waited for the serpent so that he could kill it, but he missed it. Leda hid in the bathroom. But her father wanted her to look at this serpent straight on. Her mother was opposed to this. Then her father broke down the bathroom door and Leda fainted with fright. As an epilogue, the crisis of "bodily transformation" only ended when she saw the image of a serpent curling around her and putting its head on hers. Together, they went to sleep.[2]

Puer-Oedipus

In the following clinical vignette, the puer-Oedipus expresses his permanent dreamed (symbolic) transgression in mother-son incest. Incest later involved the anima—Brigitte Bardot—and the wife of the therapist. His father has the role of an obscured and faraway Seth, but he nevertheless gives form to the final "mandala,"[3] after the old syzygic mother has been killed (this mother is likened to Tiamat, but also Cybele, the best example of the castrating woman).

> I was 26 years old in 1964, when I started analysis. At that time I held a teaching post in the country. Shortly afterward I was transferred to Paris.
>
> Feeling inhibited in all areas of my life, I decided to find the key that would open for me all the doors onto a more expansive life.
>
> This difficulty in pulling myself out of my cocoon did not

make it any easier to express what was on my mind during my analytic sessions. Luckily, dreams took the place of my own conscious expression and forced me to discuss a number of areas of my life about which, given my druthers, I would have said nothing. My dreams also presented a number of other episodes which I myself was far from being aware of, particularly those concerning my relationship with my parents.

Now perhaps certain characteristic dreams can speak for themselves about the core of my problem.

1) I am at the center of some kind of grotto, located on a sort of islet delimited by the arms of a river that is infested with crocodiles. At the center of this islet, a crowned lady— a queen—sits on a throne. It is my mother. I approach and kiss her feet. Then I caress her legs. Then a *violent desire* takes hold of me. I hold her very tightly in my arms. I cover her with kisses. I feel a very strong emotion. I also have the impression that I am not abandoning myself completely to the feeling. There is a sort of barrier, a taboo that prevents me from liberating my profound impulses.

After this embrace is over, I draw back a little. The *dead* crocodiles are floating in the river, belly up. The queen has aged quite a bit on her throne. There is nothing more to keep me here.

A few days later, like an echo to this dream, the following dreams came to me.

2) My father saw a cat in the shed. I approach the door, and the cat comes out and transfixes me with its terrible eyes. It leaps at my face to scratch out my eyes. I shield my face with my hand. I wake up suddenly, my heart beating violently.

3) I am walking on the sand, along the cliffs that hang over the beach. These cliffs are riddled with caves. Suddenly, out of one of these holes in the rock, the head of a serpent emerges. It has a scaly body and piercing eyes with something in their gaze that I can't quite define.

4) My father is coming to castrate me. He says so, and repeats it over and over. I am seized by a sudden fury. I snatch up a rod and hit him with all my strength.

5) I am having oral sex with my mother, in the same bed, and I am enjoying it. No guilty or fearful emotions at all.

6) I kiss my mother on the lips while my father is busy

talking. I do avoid doing this while my father is around, but I feel no shame.

7) I am lying down next to my mother. I kiss her neck. I complete the sex act, but this time with a strong feeling of guilt.

8) It's wartime, and I am in bed with a young woman—in this situation, she must be my mother (she was still young when my father was a prisoner, and I lived alone with her between the ages of five and six). I hold her in my arms. I complete the sex act. Everything is going very well.

9) I am in bed with my parents, between my father and my mother. I take my mother in my arms. A great feeling of well-being follows, and then ejaculation: my father is silent and obscured.

10) I take my mother in my arms. I kiss her neck. I press her against me. I have very intense feelings. A wet dream.

11) I am in bed with my mother, halfway on top of her. I hold her in my arms. A wet dream. I stay stretched out against her. I learn that my father, drunk as usual, has been found frozen where he fell asleep along the way.

12) This scene takes place in the room where my paternal grandmother used to stay, and it looks just as it did then.

My mother and Brigitte Bardot are there. I have a strange sort of sexual relationship with my mother. I lie down on the bed and "kiss" her vagina. Then I do the same with Brigitte Bardot. A painful sort of wet dream, as if some force stood in the way of ejaculation.

A few hours later, the same night:

13) In my parents' house. I am in the bedroom on the second floor, and my father is outside. I start arguing with him very violently. There is a particular violence to this, and it is going to end with some sort of one-on-one combat. I tell him explicitly that I am not afraid of him, that he can come up, that I am waiting for him on solid ground.

Having made this declaration, I am seized by doubts about the outcome of the combat. What is more, I feel guilty that I dared to engage in such a fight. Luckily, my father backs down from coming upstairs.

A few weeks later:

14) I am stretched out in bed next to my mother. She is playing the role of some kind of partner. As soon as she comes to bed, she is nude. I really want to have sex with her, but I do not dare to voice this request in words.

67

A little later in the night, I once again feel this desire to go to bed with a partner, who is once again my mother.

15) I am invited to a friend's house, and I arrive there with a pineapple pie. I am welcomed by his grandmother and her husband. We eat the pie. She tells me that her grandson has been dead for a long time. I hadn't known about that, and I do not dare ask her any questions.

Then the couple becomes my grandmother and her husband. The man, whom I don't know, becomes blurred in the dream. Then I am in bed with my grandmother. Her legs are naked. They are wrinkled. I have a strong desire to sleep with her. A wet dream.

16) I am walking with you at the seaside. It must be at Noirmoutier. We stay together for a very long time. I am very happy. You leave on urgent business: *the burial of one of your friends, also an analyst.*

Your wife and my mother meet and become friends.

There is a series of dreams where your wife takes my mother's place. Afterward—and at the same time—there is a settling of accounts with certain female characters.

17) In a medieval castle, an old woman makes life miserable for everyone. She holds the purse strings. She wants to cut off support for someone who depends on her, either her son or her husband. She goes up the stairs to join him in a room of the castle. Shortly afterward, a man comes down. We all understand that he has killed the old woman, and in any case he is not hiding it. On his way out, the man leaves two treasure chests, which he has taken back from the old woman, at the servants' disposal.

18) I am on my way to meet Aunt L. She starts to insult my *dead* mother. I grab her by the shoulders and press very hard at the base of her neck. I shake her. Since I am gripping her hands, she tries to throw me down the stairs by pushing me forward—she plans to kill me. Finally I am the one who triumphs over her. When I wake up, I have almost killed her.

This is only a very short extract from a dream series which unfolded in the course of about five years, where the patient averaged one dream per night. Dreams 1 to 15 occurred in a relatively short time: in a few months, toward the middle of treatment (the middle, only insomuch as one can assign an end to treatment).

My conclusion is again left to a dream:

> 19) I see a group of buildings that was built by my students. The body of the central building is finished. I can see, anchored onto each side of the building, the feet of the arch that will dominate the construction. (The castle of Brunehilde, in the Niebelungen, is surrounded by an identical arch.)

The same night:

> 20) My father tells me that he wants to sell our property in four parcels. He has heard about plans for a community project to reorganize the neighborhood into a circle, at the center of which will be our garden.

Notes

1. A frequent mythological theme in battles between good and evil. One example is the combat between Indra and the serpent Vritra in the Indian Rig Vedas. See also the combat between Perceval and the Red Knight, an enemy of King Arthur. Further parallels are seen in the case of the Christian Virgin cutting off the head of Satan, who has taken the form of a serpent, and in the case of Cronus, who emasculates his father Uranus.

2. A typical image of the archaic Iranian god of time, Zervan (later Mithras), with a lion's head. The serpent wrapped itself around his (human) body from the bottom all the way up, and rested its head on Zervan's lion head. Such images reflect the spiraling, cyclical time that surrounds linear, vectoral time. The time of the Mother and the time of the Father are thereby joined.

3. In Sanskrit, a magical microcosmic square or circle, an instrument of contemplation and meditation. For Jung, it was a symbol of the center, the goal, the Self as a psychic totality. It is expressed through a symmetrical arrangement of the number 4 (in a quaternity, square or circle). See dream 20 at the end of this chapter.

7

The Psychotherapist as Sacred Prostitute of Nighttime and Daytime Dreams

WE HAVE SEEN THAT IN BABYLON AND EGYPT (AS WELL as in the Near East, Asia Minor, Greece, and Rome), the festival of the New Year ended with the ritual of *hieros gamos*, a mystical union acted out by the king or priest with a sacred prostitute (hierodule). This ritual commemorated a whole series of deaths and rebirths: the death of the old year (in cyclic time) and its rebirth; the death of the son and lover (the grain god) of the Great Goddess (the Earth Mother), and his resurrection; the end of the incest of the first birth (mother-son and mother-daughter incest), and rebirth through the incest of the second birth (between sister/wife as the anima and brother/husband as the animus, and their corresponding doubles); the death of the ophidian phallus (the chthonian serpent: Kingu and Seth) of the Earth Mother, and its rebirth as the Uranian phallus (a celestial one, as in Marduk, Osiris, and Christ); the death of the toothed chthonian uterus (Tiamat and Hathor) and its rebirth as the uterus of the second birth and of eternal life (Zarpanitu, Isis, and Sophia).

The ritual of *hieros gamos* acted out two simultaneous symbolic processes: first, it was the symbolic fertilization (through imitative magic) of the new year, and of the new earth by the new grain; and second, it was the psychospiritual fertilization of the doubles and complements in eros (and eventually in caritas and agape), joining with the spirit guides of *logos spermaticos* (logos-eros) and of *logos hystericos* (eros-logos). These spirit guides were the products of the inversion-reversion of the syzygic shadow, which was both sadomasochistic and sadoparanoid (as with Tiamat-Kingu and Hathor-Seth). This inversion-reversion was achieved through the "depressive" ritual of the son god: his execution, his descent to the underworld, his solar combat against the forces of evil (or shadow) and his final resurrection, in and through his redeemed anima (examples include Zarpanitu, Isis, and Sophia—mothers regenerated and brought back to youth just like the new year and the new earth, for which they were the appropriate symbolic and imaginal representations). When this rebirth of the masculine and feminine principles (in the son god and in the mother and sister goddesses) was near completion, the *hieros gamos* joined the spiritual sides of these principles, namely the reborn doubles and complements.

As representatives of the goddess (for the hierodule) and of the god (in the case of the male prostitute), these sacred temple prostitutes worked at metamorphosing the drive into something spiritual. Therefore to unite with these divine representatives at the temple was an attempt to create an instinctual alchemy of the genital eros, a process that resembles the oral-agape instinctual alchemy that takes place in Christian communion with the body and blood of Christ.

Jung bases his theory of transference (1946) on the sixteenth century alchemical myth, *Rosarium Philosophorum*. Once again the focal point in the *Rosarium* is to experience the depressive position symbolically, in order to metabolize and integrate the previous paranoid-schizoid position and bring on the manic position of rebirth in the genital-eros register. In this alchemical myth, however, the *hieros gamos* ritual no longer marks the exit from the underworld, but instead provides an entry: the entry into death and descent to the underworld after a "loss of soul" (Solié 1980a) in order to go through the trials of dissolution, fermentation, putrefaction, and decantation (*diasparagmos*). After this passive combat with the pregenital sadomasochistic powers (a self-sacrificing acceptance), the soul, as metamorphosed or redeemed anima and animus, returns to inhabit the body of the two partners (king and queen, or the alchemist and his "mystical sister"). The two partners are thereafter united as a two-headed hermaphrodite who, once reanimated, goes on to a glorious resurrection.

The "metanoiac" theme of this passion is thus virtually the same as that of our son lovers of the Great Goddess. Only the place the *hieros gamos* occupies has changed. To be exact, the *hieros gamos* of entrance is still tainted by the drives derived from the first birth (oral incest: endocannibalism), and it is really this instinct that must be redeemed in the underworld. As for the *hieros gamos* of reemergence, it is present in the form of the reborn hermaphrodite. A sort of eternal *hieros gamos* emerges, in which the "two sexes of the spirit" (according to Michelet) are forever reunited in one complete being. Such a being may seem objectionable, and Jung does see, with good reason, its monstrous and hideous aspect (1946). In fact, this is what we call a "centrochiasmatic hermaphrodite" (Solié 1980b), one that still requires another differentiation or individuation, one above and beyond the chiasma.

Here, a diagram is more valuable than a long discourse on the subject:

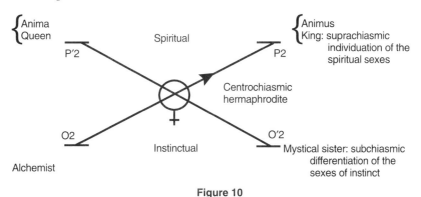

Figure 10

In fact, the centrochiasmic hermaphrodite stage stigmatizes another instinctual fusion or confusion of the "sexes of the spirit" (doubles and complements). At that point an effort is still required to distinguish between them, to individuate them in relation to the concrete object (the alchemist and the mystical sister) and in relation to objective psychic reality (archetype of the double and the complement). An effort is required to imprint the neocortex with the O2-O'2 (instinctual) and P'2-P2 (spiritual) image-objects.

Here the long work on transference takes place. Within that process the analyst plays not only the role of the alchemist and/or the mystical sister who accompanied him or her in the work, but also the king and/or queen who symbolize in alchemy the "sexes of the spirit" (eros). In other words, the analyst plays the role of sacred prostitute. What we call transference usually means the undifferentiated experience of the centrochiasmic hermaphrodite.

The following four short case vignettes demonstrate the alternation of two types of dreaming: nocturnal dreams and the daytime dreams that Jung calls "active imagination."[1]

Diana

Diana, an executive secretary who was thirty-three years old, came to treatment complaining of frigidity that made sexual pleasure and orgasm extremely difficult, except during occasional sadomasochistic rape fantasies. For eight years she had been living with a man who was thirteen years older than she, but she could not bring herself to marry him. The way she described him to me, he sounded like a son/anima willingly accepting the "hubris" and power of Diana's animus. Here is her first transference dream, which the patient reported in the third month of treatment. This will be followed by an example of active imagination, then by a dream she had in the middle of treatment, and finally by her latest dream.

> I am here [in my office], at the table. You are next to me, and you are showing me necklaces of African pearls. I unstring them one by one like a rosary, or rather like the days which separate me from each of our sessions. I count them.
> Your knee is against mine and you put your arm around my shoulders. "Let me go!" I tell you. You take your arm away,

and we go on unstringing and threading the pearls. I see pictures of naked women with wounded and bleeding vaginas (as in African initiations). I believe that you have betrayed my confidence. What I wanted to find in you was a mother.

Now the room is empty and sad. A woman in black goes to your desk and starts giving orders [as Diana does in her work]. You call a client on the phone and then you start laughing. It is too much for me, I feel abandoned.

But suddenly I look at your face, and I see that it isn't you at all. The man who is taking your place is pretentious, mean, coldly logical . . . And so there is still hope for my relationship with you. Even so, I wake up crying.

Diana was depressed for many months, during which she had fantasies in dreams and in active imagination about being swallowed up by the sea or by the earth, about conflicts, about dismemberments endured or imposed on others, and about both hetero- and homosexual sodomizations. After two and a half years of analysis, she experienced the following fantasy (active imagination):[2]

We [she and I] are together in my bed. An enormous green snake, several meters long, comes to talk to me. He approaches me, twines himself around me, and then unwraps himself—this is very pleasurable for us. He comes in the same way every night, and now I always wait for him naked.

Now, this green snake has a twin brother, who is black and nasty—he terrifies me. He sticks his head in the door from time to time and threatens to come in. The black one is venomous, unlike his brother. I have the feeling that a struggle between the two brothers is not far behind.

The next day, I make love with the green snake, and it's wonderful. I start doing it again every night. Then one night he arrives, touches me, rolls and unrolls himself, penetrates me, and then withdraws afterwards. As he stretches himself out on top of me, I meet his eyes. I scream, horrified: it is the black snake, disguised as the green one, who had just taken his brother's place. Yes, now I can see that his color is deeper, while the other snake had been more glowing. He tells me that he has killed his brother but that I don't have to be so afraid, that he will treat me better than his brother. He wants to teach me the right way to make love. Then he sodomizes me. I end up enjoying this and reaching such true orgasm that I completely forget the poor green snake . . .

Then one day I hear crying in the street. It comes from a garbage can. I look inside and there I find the green snake: imprisoned, sick, emaciated, raving with fever, shrunken . . . I feel ashamed. I ask him what he is doing there. And he answers, "The soul is eternal."

In my sexual fantasies you (the analyst) have also sodomized me. And I felt ashamed, because I had soiled you, destroyed you.

An intermediate dream took the following form:

I go to my parents' house. There I am introduced to a middle-aged man. I notice that he has black eyes (like yours). I hear that he knows how to do everything, including everything sexual. Since I am attracted to him, I decide to try him out.

He is a little slow in understanding what I want. So I help him undress. While we are making love, he starts talking. I make him shut up.[3] It's just because I really want it to work this time. And in fact I manage for the first time to feel an intense orgasm.

Later, my mother comes to see me in the kitchen. She is upset. The furniture has been moved. She learns that my daughter [Diana has no children] has decided not to go to her review course in geography. I think: Why should she go? She has learned her lessons regularly. My daughter is definitely becoming more and more independent.

Diana sporadically continued to fight the sadomasochistic syzygy (symbolized by Tiamat and the black snake). One day, she told me of her upcoming marriage to her friend (whom we will call Hippolytus[4]), which has since been consummated.

Diana's last transference dream took the following shape:

I am at Pierre Solié's home, on the top floor of a modern building. I am in a vast room which is lit by large bay windows. Pierre Solié says to me: "Remember your earlier dreams, where there were two animus figures. We have only talked about the first one, but it is the second one which is important. At the time, it had a disturbing air about it." I recall this dream again.

Pierre Solié slides into bed next to me. He is naked, but it isn't him, it's Hippolytus.

But he just keeps talking while I put my hand on his thigh: "The two wings have just descended into your body. Make sure you keep it closed so that they don't escape." And I say to myself: "But that means he believes it this time!" I am skeptical. I only feel death.

Certainly the alchemist's *nigredo*, or descent into the underworld, had not fully ended for Diana. At that point she still felt only this symbolic death and the skepticism (nihilism) that went along with it. But it is there that rebirth exists. It also exists in my own transference (and not only countertransference, as Fedida (1978) has emphasized so well), which had accompanied Diana all along and that continues to accompany her on this painful journey.

Daphne

Daphne, a thirty-five-year-old psychologist with four children, also had enormous difficulty with feeling sexual pleasure and practically never had an orgasm. As for sexual desire, it couldn't be set free in her except after a real dousing with alcohol, which as everyone knows "dissolves" the superego. Diana could only reach orgasm with the help of sadomasochistic and/or homosexual fantasies of a sexual threesome with her husband and another woman.[5]

The first transference dream did not appear until the fourteenth month of her analysis. It was very short: "You are a woman, a rather masculine one." Inasmuch as my relationship with Diana was lived out with my psychological sex double, her own animus, so my transferential relationship with Daphne was lived out with my psychological sex complement, my anima—which was her own double. The second dream also displays this psychological sex double: "I am lying here on your couch, and I

77

am sleeping. Meanwhile my sister," (whom we will call Echo, to stay among the nymphs) "who came here at the same time I did, is talking to you and settling some important problems. I am jealous that no one is paying attention to me anymore."

The third dream hardly changes register: "I come back to your office. The couch has moved. It is in the corner. There is a table and you are behind it with a girl." The fourth dream fits into this progression: "I am in a big bed and I ask you to kiss me. You become a woman. We have to talk about desire in a religious group where, appropriately enough, it is forbidden."

As an adolescent in a religious school, Daphne had had an "erotic-mystical" homosexual episode with her teacher, a nun—this was strictly a fantasy. But this "special friendship" was important in her life and in her analysis.

I would be changed into a woman again in many other dreams—just like Leucippus in the legend of Daphne. And during these scenes there would be exhibitionistic images of all kinds flashing by, especially scatological bathroom imagery.

It was not until the fifth year of work that the following dream could emerge:

> I come in for psychoanalysis. Before me you are seeing one of my divorced friends who has enormous problems. I am comparing myself to her—she has two children and works for minimum wage and basically has all kinds of problems which are much more important than mine. It seems that she is in love with my husband. I am saying to myself that I could let her take my place—in analysis, not in my marriage—but it's not really an option. In fact, it wasn't you who was there, but a substitute. I am not happy about this, but I lie down on the couch anyway. He tells me to talk. I don't feel very confident.
>
> And suddenly he splits in two. He has his head on one side and the rest of his body on the other side. It is this remainder, this other, which suddenly throws himself on top of me, kisses me (theoretically without a head), abuses me, turns me over and rapes me savagely . . . from behind . . . in the anus. I feel this and I reach a very intense climax.
>
> Then "they" disappear—the head and the other part—and I find myself alone, my underwear stained with blood as if I had just had sex for the first time. I am alone with this

underwear, in the middle of a street. The underwear is dragging on the ground, and I want to pick it up and hide it . . .
But someone else grabs it before I do. I run after this person. I catch up. It is a little girl. She rips off my diamond
with a little knife, saying she won't give my underwear back.
She breaks my diamond. Then I am more worried about the
diamond than about the underwear.

But suddenly I am completely disgusted, thinking of that
sleazy guy who disappeared so quickly after finishing the act.
I was purely a sex object for him—and what an object!

Here we have a beautiful example of temple prostitution—
part of the alchemical system we have been working with. Even
the "anal" diamond has to be broken to prepare for the arrival of
the "genital" diamond—and then of caritas.

This genital diamond was not slow in forming during the
following weeks. A dream from this period: "You are with me in a
room where there is a clock with no hands. We are outside of
time and space." And outside of good and evil as well.

Another dream:

I go to church with my husband—we are going to meet
you there. At first there is a woman analyst there, but I don't
want to talk to her. I hear you telling me to hurry. And I go
with you.

In her life now, she experiences sexual desire and pleasure,
including orgasm—even ecstasy—when she has sex with her husband. She has also lost the extra pounds that used to weigh down
her bulimic "flesh" as compensation. One of her last dreams:

I give birth to brown-haired children—my own children
are all blond. I wasn't expecting it. It just happened, just like
that. I figured my birth control must have failed. I go to see
the gynecologist, who assures me that my birth control de-
vice was working just fine.

The symbolic child can surpass the constraints of birth control
devices.

At the temples there were male prostitutes, who were certainly meant for women, but also for homosexuals. I could pass

along at this point one of the most beautiful love letters that I have ever received, which was from a homosexual.

But along with homosexuals who are inverted or "hyperverted," there are also hermaphrodites.[6] This term describes us all, since to some degree or another we all have a dose of latent homosexuality.

Acteon

Acteon, a forty-five-year-old engineer, had the peculiar habit of choosing as his mates only the Artemis types who, as we know, cause him to be eaten by his own dogs, only to disappear afterward. I will limit myself to quoting just the key dream of his analysis:

> We [he and I] are together. At your suggestion, we go to bed together, to have "an experience" . . . what experience?, I wonder.
>
> I take off my pajama bottoms, like with Artemis [the most recent one "in service"].
>
> You come and curl up against my left shoulder, just like Artemis does. I tell you: "You're so heavy . . . I have never been with a *woman* who weighed this much . . ." I even have the impression that you are making yourself heavier on purpose. But after all, I tell myself, this must be normal, since he is a man.
>
> A woman—another analyst—is present during this experience. She is attentive, very friendly and animated.
>
> I feel like telling you both my sexual and spiritual reactions.
>
> Then you tell me: "Now you are ready to find a woman."
>
> The woman analyst adds: "Yes, he's doing very well."
>
> I agree that I will be a good husband or a perfect companion and that I know many ways to please a woman.
>
> Then we try to get up, but we get tangled in the sheets.
>
> We are afraid that we have gone past the forty-five minutes allotted for the analytic hour.
>
> I lower my shirt to cover my penis, which is in a state of major erection.[7]

I would not invent a dream like this. And, believe it or not, Acteon took a whole year to figure out and digest the meaning of the "experience" involved in this dream's analytic hour. Patience is the major virtue of the modern sacred prostitute.[8]

Olympias

Olympias,[9] a forty-three-year-old teacher, has three children by different fathers. Only the first of her children's fathers actually lived with her for a few years. The two others were casual lovers, which she continues to have, often many at once. Her sexual and affective instability made her particularly susceptible to all types of paranoiacs, heads of various cults—the kind of people who these days are fighting over the schizoids of the planet.

After three years of analysis (the first two with a woman analyst) Olympias finally freed herself from the last of these "devouring" lovers. During that time she was stuck in a depressive state, and she wrote me the following letter between two sessions (she would often write to me because she lived far from Paris):

> I'm doing very badly, I have never been so bad . . . I am regressing so much that you shouldn't be surprised if I go back to the abyss from which I emerged. I no longer enjoy anything, not even masturbating, and yet I developed a full-blown fantasy through which I could once more enter the arms of our Great Mother, if only for a few moments. Here it is:
> The ceremony takes place in a temple, by candlelight. You make me lie down on some kind of altar, and the worshippers form a semicircle. It is necessary for the worshippers to include my parents, A and B [her current lovers], and sometimes also my brothers and sisters or my children. Your role is to cut out my clitoris. You bind me to the table without tying my hands, because I have to masturbate in front of everyone; you are the one who chooses when to perform the operation, and I don't know whether or not you have decided to let me reach orgasm one last time before you start. Sometimes, to speed up the process, you let one of

my lovers come forward and caress me with his tongue. My parents, who are being forced to attend this ceremony, are filled with indignation and disgust. When you feel that the orgasm is taking too long, you whip me and then slowly push your finger into the unprotected hole which leads to the fertile Cavern. After your finger moves back and forth a few times, I start writhing and screaming with pleasure . . . So loudly that you forget what you're supposed to be doing!

I long only for this mother, into whose bosom I want to dissolve; my desire for love is truly the desire for that. But then what am I going to be left with? I am struggling against a hellish power, that sucks me down to the bottom of the pit, toward nothingness.

I asked her to establish a dialogue[10] with the serpent,[11] and here is the result:

First Dialogue (November 19)
"Who are you, serpent?"
"I am your helping spirit, and that of your analyst, just as I used to be a helping spirit for many shamans. I am what you were thousands of years ago and what you are still: the part of yourself that is most animalistic, your instinctive self. I am as old as the world and I have experienced many things and gone through many changes. With me, you must be who you are; I can do a lot for you if you accept this dialogue.

"I am the caterpillar, you are the butterfly. A butterfly who mistakes itself for a bull, and who believes because of this that it won't be able to cross the bars behind which it believes itself to be imprisoned. In order for you to become what you are, I have accepted my state of being as a serpent. So you, too, must accept the task of being what you are, nothing more and nothing less. Once you achieve that, you will be able to fly away toward the light. Look, the spaces between your prison bars are wide enough to allow a whole cloud of butterflies your size to go out together. The sun is about to rise, and it feels good to fly in the open air. Don't hold back."

"It must be delicious, to be the butterfly you're talking about, but I am afraid of being that fragile."

"It is necessary to accept it all, to completely accept the

fragility, the precariousness of your condition. Once you have done that, you will be able to enjoy the light."

"Serpent, why do you insist that I talk to you?"

"I am responsible for teaching you, and believe me, it is an extraordinary opportunity for you to be taught by the serpent that I am. Since your earliest childhood, I have been preparing you for this communication with me. Think back to that cult in which you spent several years, and to the way in which the man you saw as your master forced you, under pain of death, to dialogue with him inside you. Thanks to that earlier formation, now you are able to hear me and speak to me directly. You do ultimately realize how simple it is, and you are very special to me, since few other people would voluntarily agree to speak to a serpent this way."

"I've had it up to here with all that. I am no longer looking for a special honor or mission. I only want one thing: peace."

"Unfortunately you have no choice: you will have to accomplish what has been predestined."

"It's strange . . . all that time when I was looking for, hoping for, this type of dialogue, I absolutely could not manage to find it—and yet, what wouldn't I have given then, for the privilege of contacting a spirit? And now that I am no longer interested in it, the contact has finally been established . . ."

"It is precisely because you no longer hope for anything of the kind that you are ready for it now."

"Serpent, what is the connection between you and my analyst?"

"I inspire him in his writing, because I am the phallus of the Earth Mother and also her uterus, her hollow organ."

"Please let me rest, I have a headache—it is so tiring to meet with you."

Second Dialogue (November 20)

"Serpent, why do you forbid me to reach orgasm with anyone other than you?"

"You will understand that little by little as you put it into practice. For years you have wanted to practice tantric yoga, but you haven't been able to do it because you have had no partner or guru. Now I am offering to be both for you. Pay close attention to what I am saying: it would be dangerous for you to transgress, not to take me seriously. From now on, you will only be able to reach orgasm with my participation.

For this it will be necessary for me to enter you according to the ritual which is familiar to you. That will work with A and with C [one of the two previous lovers has now been replaced by another]. For the time being I will not often visit you while C is there, but don't worry: while you are deprived of orgasm, you will instead be filled with a different kind of pleasure."

"But C might think that I'm frigid, that bothers me."

"You can simulate your pleasure when it is necessary for his, and you won't have any trouble with that because contact with him will send you into a feeling of bliss."

Third Dialogue (November 21)

"Serpent, I think you are the one from whom I feel so distant right now. I have the impression that something in me has changed."

"Yes, you accept me at last, you even desire me. Now we will be able to live together on good terms and do the work we have to do together."

"What will that be?"

"The realization of your origins, so that, once you are solidly grounded, you will be able to look at the sky without feeling dizzy."

"Who am I?"

"You have the impression of being locked in a prison. In reality, you are in a room covered with mirrors: all that you see, which you think is on the outside, is actually inside you.

"The prison bars are inside you, and so are the sky and space. They are in you and they are you. When you understand that the outside world does not exist, you will no longer try to escape from your supposed prison; instead you will continue to carefully examine the mirrors, to learn to understand yourself."

"And I suppose that at that moment I won't see the bars anymore?"

"Oh no, that's the only way to get through the bars!"

"I think that I have just begun to understand something very important."

"You know that when you dream, the characters in the dream represent parts of yourself. And so reality is like dreaming in that sense."

"So you're saying that when I see someone in front of me, I am really seeing a part of myself?"

"How could it be otherwise? Everyone has a complete inability to perceive anything but himself."

"That's terrible: does that mean that each of us is completely alone?"

"Yes, but multiple in nature! . . ."

"I will never be able to leave my own universe and enter someone else's?"

"No."

"And so I'm alone?"

"Yes, but why should that bother you? You are as vast as your universe, and so as vast as the Universe. You are the human being in its totality."

"This vision leaves me feeling dizzy and perplexed."

Fourth Dialogue (November 23)

"Hello, Serpent! What do you have to tell me?"

"Greetings, Olympias . . . Unfortunately for us, a woman once crushed my head. You, on the other hand, with your love, have allowed my head to enter the center of your insides, and for that I thank you . . . Your analyst is letting me do good work. My voice makes him docile, and he resists my suggestions less and less now. I have chosen him carefully. With the "S" in his last initial, I am at the head of his name. I have given him "Pierre" as a first name because serpents like to hide themselves under such rocks. But there is an "L" missing at the end of his name—if it were "Soliel," then he could be for me the Sun I need for my transformation. This "L" would also be the wing that would allow him to fly.[12] With your help, Olympias, I will give it to him, and allow him to make use of it."

"What do you mean by that?"

"Think back to a dream you had last year, where you visited him and he told you that you would have a job to do together. You have now undertaken a mission in which you will really be the guide."

"Missions don't interest me anymore, grand as they may be. I no longer want anything but peace."

Shortly after this fourth dialogue, Olympias arrived for her session one day in a state of inflation, a state of being possessed by "serpent power" (Avalon 1977). She sat in my usual chair and indicated that I should take the couch. With a little smile, I accepted this role reversal—I sat on the couch, but without lying down. I let pass a long moment of silence, and then feeling— both of us—that the fate of the treatment lay in that moment, I started to tell her, with many more details than I have provided here, the beautiful story of the two Aztec serpents Quetzalcoatl and Tezcatlipoca.

At the end of the story, she looked at me, smiling, relaxed, "unswollen." She was happy that I had been able to accept the power of her serpent without abdicating the power of my own serpent, thereby uniting the two.

From then on, a face-to-face dialogue began—or almost face-to-face. Here is her last letter:

> I feel like coming to the end of therapy now. I think this is the right time.
>
> I remember the state I was in at the beginning: awash in suffering and completely disoriented.
>
> One short year has been enough to make me into a completely unrecognizable person. Now I am finally happy to be alive, and I also have the feeling of standing solidly on my own two feet!
>
> I am realizing how much my contact with C is doing me good, allowing my animus to be harmoniously integrated. I used to believe it was impossible to meet someone who would respond so well to my needs. I feel that I am truly overflowing, and I can really see the changes in me: for example, I feel a great burst of love for others and an intense desire to understand them. My attitude toward my son is changing. I used to feel a great indifference toward him, and now he seems worthy of love. Now I want him to continue his studies, although in October I had told him just the opposite. I have decided, to his great joy, that he will no longer be in boarding school next year, but that he should go to a local high school.
>
> I feel an enthusiasm and a taste for trying all kinds of things.
>
> The pill which I was forced to go back on no longer gives me so much trouble—on the contrary, it has an antibulimic effect on me, and overall it is quite beneficial to me.
>
> My overly introverted attitude is changing into a better sense of equilibrium: I am surprised to find myself interested in the outside world. I have even considered getting a

television! Not so much for the programs themselves, but so that I can keep up with what interests other people. I even feel the need to listen to the news every day!

I feel like my center of gravity has shifted. Now I can say: everything tells me that being connected to my own center also connects me to the center of the world. My wish, the one expressed so well by the card from C which I showed you, is finally being realized. Of course, I have no illusions; the time I have left to live will hardly be enough to accomplish my task, but the biggest part of the work has been done.

Notes

1. A technique perfected by Jung using his own fantasies. It consists of bringing to life and living out as much as possible, in the imaginary, images of emotions, affects, desires, and love. See Jung (1961) and Humbert (1984).

2. Which could be entitled "Quetzalcoatl and Tezcatlipoca," after two enemy Aztec gods. They took the form of serpents; Quetzalcoatl, who had wings, gave birth to humanity through his mouth.

3. Freud interfered a bit less after a patient once asked him to shut up.

4. Diana gathered up this son of Theseus, who was murdered by his stepmother Phaedra and brought back to life by the doctor Asclepius.

5. Diana is a "daughter animus," a powerful psychological sex complement, while Daphne is a "daughter anima," an important psychological sex double.

6. The invert is the man/woman or the woman/man. The hypervert is the super-male or super-female, who are homosexual. See Solié (1980b).

7. Let me emphasize that this "major" erection implies that there are "minor" erections.

8. Not every analysis develops this way, thank God!

9. Wife of Philip of Macedonia, and mother of Alexander the Great. She had been a hierodule at Eleusis and claimed that the father of her son was actually the serpent of the mysteries. Philip took offense at this.

10. This is an example of active imagination. The author intends to illustrate the value of active imagination and seems to assume that, if the reader follows the interplay of images within Olympias and between her and the analyst, his point could be understood intuitively. Olympias first has to take a step beyond passive daydreams and seemingly idle

(masturbatory) sexual fantasies in order to free herself from the regressive pull of the Great Mother. She then engages in active imagination which facilitates the personification of autonomous psychic forces, in order to lead the ego into dialogue with them (such as she does with the serpent). This dialogue helps the ego gain a greater degree of "subjectivity" and to de-identify from overwhelming psychic forces by conferring upon them a greater measure of objectivity, thereby releasing the psyche's healing potential. As a result of the use of active imagination within the context of her analysis, Olympias experiences a shift in attitude (a move away from the schizoid world within which she had heretofore been ensconced), as evidenced by a greater capacity to relate to the inner and outer worlds and to others, her son in particular. (R.G.J.)

11. Presumably Olympias previously encountered this serpent in dreams or in fantasy. (editor's note)

12. The serpent's word games make more sense in French. *Pierre*, the author's first name, is also French for "rock." The word for sun is *soleil*, a word similar to the serpent's transformation of the author's surname. *Aile*, pronounced like the letter *L*, means "wing"; therefore, adding an *L* to the author's last name would be like giving it wings. (translator's note)

8

Geo-History: Political, Imaginary, and Therapeutic

THE FOLLOWING TWO CASE STUDIES DEMONSTRATE mobilization and "negotiation" of paranoid-schizoid fantasies through a Manichean projection onto world political events, past or present. The first case (Adolf) is clearly borderline (pre-genital). The second case (Demosthenes) is more hysterical (genital).

Adolf

Adolf, a thirty-one-year-old history teacher, was referred to me because he felt persecuted by his students, which led him to make endless paranoid interpretations. He squeezed himself into a corner of the couch, his eyes fixed on his folded hands. When he answered questions, it was only with a certain trailing off, with a yes or no, and then he would lift his eye to quickly scan the place from which my voice emanated, immediately plunging his gaze back down to the turning movement of his two thumbs in his lap. This is how Adolf presented himself, even though in the course of our sessions he told me that he was the son of a railway worker who nevertheless had barely missed getting into the finest university in France; he based a profound resentment on this one failure.

Adolf's father had died five years before. He lived with his mother in the miserable little apartment where he had spent his whole life. No emotion, no feeling at all, showed in his clipped speech, which was ripped with great effort from a body that seemed somehow foreign to him. Sexually, his life was "aphanisis"[1]: complete nothingness.

Adolf reported no dreams. Only after thirty sessions with him did I see him get a bit animated when I asked him a historical question. Little by little he confided in me that he spent his days—and a good part of his nights—imagining battles worthy of Alexander the Great, Julius Caesar, Napoleon . . . or Hitler. Everything was there, in the most minute detail, from the uniform of a common soldier down to the last button of the general's jacket, from the foot soldiers to the artillery, passing through the commissary on the way. The geography of the places, which he drew on maps, was absolutely faithful to the borders of each period in question. The armies were laid out according to a strategy, and they operated according to tactics so impressive that later on I found myself checking to see whether some of these battles had actually taken place. Some of the battles lasted as long as six months.

Adolf's geography progressively limited itself to one region of France, the Seine-et-Marne. This region had been attacked and invaded by a barbarian from the east, then reduced to the most abject slavery. He described sadistic scenes perpetrated on the native population, which showed an incredibly refined cruelty. The Seine-et-Marne cycle lasted two years. Spectator and leader in this game, Adolf sometimes acted it out—in his imagination—but he was always on the side of the conquered and the tortured, describing his tortures at those moments with an emotional pleasure[2] to which was added a certain exhibitionism of his gaping wounds.

Of course, Seine-et-Marne is the home of his mother's family.

The east, for him, is the classic source of barbaric invasions, but also of nazism and communism. The east is the father, one might say, with a perfect manifestation of the "primal scene." Yes, but the answer is not that simple. This father figure, united to the mother in "sadistic intercourse," is not completely the father, but instead the famous "incorporated penis" in the mother's body. In other words, as we have seen, it was the animus of the mother. The father—at least the symbolic father (in Lacan's terms)—had not gone through his true "epiphany." Here we are still in the domain of archaic syzygy (the first oedipal stages, according to Klein—the "combined parents"). Adolf identified himself in a fusional way with the tortured body of his mother (Tiamat-Kingu) and projected his own sadism onto the barbarian (phallic bad object: Marduk), which he tried to separate from the mother through war—because fighting means separation. However, Adolf, unlike the hero Marduk, had never succeeded in achieving this separation from the mother's body. Nazism and communism for him were other signifiers of this sadism.

And so we find ourselves in the true Tartarus, the chthonian (underground) domain par excellence. The persecuting students—all male—were representatives of this Marduk, which Adolf's projected sadism transformed into a bloody phallus that divides, rapes, and dismembers. But instead of fighting, Adolf was thrown down like Kingu,[3] avoiding eye contact and exhibiting his wounds to others' eyes. He offered an attitude that emanated from the "female," situated at the crossroads of seduction, fascination, sensuality, and terror.

Adolf gradually began to identify with the sadistic invader. At this point the feelings of external persecution had long ago ceased. The themes that had been awakened in his dreams diminished little by little. He could imagine resuming his work by making educational television shows. One day, after five years of treatment, he declared that he had "nothing more to do here." I heard from him recently. He will remain for the most part an invalid because of his first "castration" by the toothed vagina of the first birth, but the "stump" seems to be scarred over.

Demosthenes

Demosthenes, a twenty-four-year-old bank administrator, came to see me for speech problems that were the result of a stammer. He also sought treatment for sexual problems that had clearly gotten worse for the last two years, until he had reached a state of almost complete impotence. Paradoxically, his verbal expression had begun to improve just then.

His mother was anxious to the point of obsession and smothered her children like "a gas fixture." His father was so absorbed in his work that he never learned to drive a car and thus left the "stick" to his wife. An older brother had some trouble involving himself in life.

Demosthenes was seeing a childhood friend, Agrippa, who fascinated him by becoming the girlfriend of the son of the man he suspected (fantasized) was his mother's lover.

Two recurring dream images marked this stage of his treatment: one of a gigantic explosion (possibly atomic) from which he awoke in terrified anguish, and one of a woman's genitals sectioned longitudinally, whose two parts moved about in the air, separated by an impenetrable grille.

A phobic fantasy of his consisted of the fear of castrating himself while sleepwalking (his brother was a sleepwalker), which he related to another rather frequent dream in which he cut a snake to ribbons. In yet another recurrent dream, he put his head into a vagina in which he discovered a swarm of snakes. So he plunged his hand inside, pulled out a nest of vipers, and threw it away from him while shooting at it with a gun.

Sometimes in dreams he climbed up a cliff, only to fall onto the sand, which cushioned his fall. There he turned into a woman and gave birth to a child.

Or else Agrippa's vagina was suddenly very strange. It had no pubic hair, but instead something more like quills; it looked like a purse, or rather like a sea urchin's mouth, with a depression in the middle like an anus.

Sometimes he made love with his mother while Agrippa sat on his mother's chest.

Later he found himself in his parents' garden, where he fell in love with his sister [he doesn't have a sister]. The sister up until then had been completely indifferent toward him. It was an amazing feeling. They pledged to love each other for the rest of their lives. They kissed furiously. There remained just the problem of how to deal with the "guy" she had been living with. The mother walked in on them but this didn't bother them at all.

The anima/sister (a complement): did she pick up where the mother left off? His mother, out of those vagina Demosthenes saw a snake emerging, which had not yet come all the way out, used to tell him that when the babies (his brother and he) moved during her pregnancies, she had had the impression that there was a snake in her belly.

A little later, the analytic hour took place in his parents' apartment, with his parents present, along with his mother's presumed lover. The mother looked at the notes I was taking and connected what I had written to the image of the father, and she had as a double this man whom she had erotically cathected, who therefore possessed the phallus that she recognized in him.

With another boy, Demosthenes had planned to make love to a girl but they lost their erections. So she first made love to another boy, then to him, always with her on top. She had an orgasm but he didn't. Then she stroked him with her hand and he had a very violent orgasm, all the time blushing so much that the other boy and the girl asked him if he was faking it. A second girl came along, who did not find all this to be terribly moral.

In short, everything was doubled and somewhat inverted for Demosthenes. Meanwhile, in reality, he could only make love when Agrippa took the top position. The fantasies that helped him realize this were exactly those involving a foursome of two doubles (he and his double) and two complements (the partner and his anima). Here we see the reprise of the alchemical foursome and the crossover of mythological motifs involving son lovers and Great Mother goddesses.

Another aphrodisiacal fantasy that began in Demosthenes' early adolescence—and which he still thought about while masturbating during this time—is one of a girl trapped in a cave, whom he ties up and holds under his absolute slavish domination. No chains, no whips, no instruments of torture—just the cord, the contention, the absolute mastery of this dangerous femininity, "the dark continent."

During this time—a period of five years—Demosthenes'

speech problems completely disappeared, and he conquered his impotence, still with great effort, using these techniques. He married Agrippa and had a son with her, but he did not have a job worthy of him. What is more, a writing cramp took the place of his verbal and sexual castrations. At one point he could not even manage to write his own signature—which, for a banker, is an overwhelming handicap.

During a trip to Berlin, he was fascinated by the wall of shame, the Iron Curtain. It suddenly reminded him of his dream about the impenetrable grille separating the two parts of the split vagina. For two years after that he piled up image after image of the modern world as being divided in two. He gave me a whole schema of these divisions, briefly summarized here.

Everything begins in Germany, which is always reborn from its ashes like a phoenix or a dragon.

In the third and fourth centuries, Germany, along with some pagans from southern Denmark, invaded Roman England. After that there were battles with the Normans, but the Saxons were the first to found a political class in ancient England.

The Anglo-Saxons emigrated to America during the Renaissance and the process of colonization extended west all the way to California. It was the Saxons, with the Teutonic knights, who, in the thirteenth century, emigrated east, toward the Slavs. Until the fifteenth and sixteenth centuries, Russia was just a tiny state that was continually ravaged by the Mongols and the Tartars. Russia only became a great state by relying on the German spirit. It was Peter the Great, and then Catherine II, a German princess who assassinated her husband, who made Russia the great European power that it is. It was the Germans who established Russia's first industrial movements.

Thus the Saxons and Germany were the Great Mothers who spilled out their children to the West and to the East.

In the seventeenth and eighteenth centuries, Russia conquered Siberia while the Americans conquered the west coast of the Pacific.

Finally, it was the same men (brothers) who, on the left and on the right sides, spilled out toward the two edges of the Pacific. But they lost all contact. They were radically split in two.

One of the two camps conquered California and founded a leading-edge industry there. A valley there became the seat of all the great industries. And from there, this industry nourished Japan, who took over (along with South Korea, where three companies had the biggest rates of expansion in 1977).

The other camp conquered the forests of frozen Siberia, and there created its own leading-edge industries. From there, it also nourished—by its ideas anyway—China and the other communist countries of the Far East.

Let's compare this phenomenon to a piece of gum being pulled in opposite directions: the center stretches out and finally collapses. Once these people had left Germany, the twentieth century depression came along in the Germanic world. Similarly, a spiritual depression emerged among Christians, which was paralleled by the appearance of Jewish genius (as evidenced by Marx, Einstein, and Freud), but also by the Nazi countermovement. Hitler saw himself as the savior—a demonic savior—of the Christian world, which was being crushed beneath the boot of the communist world, a world that had arisen from Germany (in West Germany and Eastern Europe). Today, capitalism and Marxism are having trouble in the countries where they started out, while they are proliferating in the Oriental countries which they have enriched. Even China and Japan have now made agreements with each other, and the "yellow threat" is more than ever the order of the day in our economic war.

But meanwhile old Europe has been recovering and seeking agreements with the Oriental countries. The East-West reunion took place once more through a North-South meeting, the depression in Central Europe reached its peak, the cut was healed, the *coniunctio oppositorum* was achieved. The two separate parts of the genitals of Great Mother Europe were reunited at last. And so Demosthenes' schema ultimately signifies this reunion, made in symbol and thus also in meaning.

He just found a job commensurate with his abilities and is living with a satisfied Agrippa and with a son who is flourishing wonderfully.

Notes

1. Absence of sexual desire.
2. The word Solié uses for pleasure, *jouissance*, was discussed exten-

sively by Jacques Lacan, and it has been used by theorists in numerous fields since then. As used by the medieval troubadours, *jouissance* meant much more than sexual pleasure, suggesting in addition more general emotional processes, such as the feeling of achieving a fulfilled wholeness. Solié is no doubt alluding to the work of Lacan and others when he uses this rich poetic term. (translator's note)

3. Or the lunar Marduk, or Osiris.

9

Therapeutic Literature

PSYCHOTHERAPY, EVEN THE ANALYTICAL VARIETY, IS AN art for a jack-of-all-trades; at its best, it is a craft. Like a fire, it makes do with all kinds of woods. Here literature has a contribution, starting with the *Memoirs* of President Schreber.

President Schreber

The case of Daniel Paul Schreber,[1] "God's prostitute" (Levy 1976), shows certain similarities with our case study of Adolf, and even with that of Demosthenes. In President Schreber's case, delusional discourse goes much farther than in the other two cases because castration, which is intended to change him into a woman, is expressed openly. It allows us to witness a sexual pleasure and sensuality approaching mystical bliss.

Schreber, to refer to him more simply, at first displayed a hypochondriacal delusion, then a delusion of persecution, of which the object was first his doctor, Professor Flechsig, and finally God in person. Only when the persecuting object passed from man to God could the patient give free rein to his most radical inversion, an inversion of sex.

Castration here takes the meaning of a "tendency, innate in the Order of the World," to demand the "unmanning" of whoever has been admitted into intimate and permanent interaction with the rays (of God) (Schreber 1955, pp. 72-73). "Blessedness"[2] (the "orgasm of God's nerves") explodes into a sensation of the sharpest sensuality.

The emasculation here takes place in such a way that the masculine genitals retract inside the belly. A concurrent deformation of these newly internal genital organs changes them to their feminine counterparts: "For weeks I was kept in bed and my clothes were removed to make me—as I believed—more amenable to voluptuous sensations, which could be stimulated in me by the female nerves which had already started to enter my body . . ." (Schreber 1955, p. 76). First his body was subjected to being "prostituted like that of a female harlot" (Schreber 1955, p. 99), and then he could be fertilized by the divine rays for the purpose of generating a new race of men, the race he called "new human beings out of Schreber's spirit." From then on, Schreber dedicated himself to the "worship of the feminine." In thirteen years (between 1883 and 1900), his body was completely transformed into a woman's, "God's woman," immersed in a sensual ravishment: "I have to imagine myself as man and woman in one person having intercourse with myself" (Schreber 1955, p. 208). What a magnificent description of narcissistic *uroborus* (a snake eating its own tail) and of second-generation syzygy (an anal syzygy), the erotic-heroic (*hieros gamos*) theme of all the son lovers. Schreber set himself up at once as the mother of a new race and as a "prostitute of God."

He was a sacred prostitute, whom Georges Bataille (1986) describes as the consecration of transgression: "In her, the sacred aspect, the forbidden aspect of the sexual does not hesitate to appear: her entire life is devoted to the violation of the forbidden."

"God would never attempt to withdraw," Schreber continues, ". . . If I could *always* rest my gaze on female beings . . . if I could *always* look at female pictures" (1955, p. 210).

Without a doubt, seen from the viewpoint of delusion, the man's femininity is shown to be sacred pleasure, sensuality, and bliss in the uninterrupted fusion (syzygy) that leads to death— for the purpose of gaining eternal life.

But, what do you think of the Schreberian God, particularly in relation to Adolf's barbarian or to the God discussed later in this chapter?

Don Juan

Just as Schreber tends toward absolute sensuality, so Don Juan— the provocateur of God, the "woman's whore"[3]—loses himself in absolute provocation and pride. At every moment, he must prove to himself that God is dead, that he has killed Him. "It is a matter between Heaven and me," affirms Molière's Don Juan to his falsely innocent valet Sganarelle, "and we will work it out quite well together without you worrying about it." Each feminine conquest is a transgression in which the impunity of the hero frees him from divine alienation.

"The true pleasure of love consists in its variety" (Molière 1876, p. 73).

Don Juan takes exactly the counterstance to the eternal divine and to the permanence of legalized love—that of his wife Elvira, in particular. He refuses to imitate this divine and legalistic eternity like a trained monkey. He must constantly sink into the heart of the unknown, to find something new: "I have in this the ambition of conquerors, who go from victory to victory, and cannot bring themselves to put limits to their longings" (ibid.).

"What canst thou keep?" asks the Devil of Edouard Rostand's Don Juan.

"What Alexander's dust/ has kept, the joy of knowing that it was/ Almighty Alexander! Only, I/ Am all my army, and 'tis I myself/ That have possessed!" (Rostand 1929, p. 44).

Of course, here again is the struggle of the hero whose rivalry results not only from the "penis" incorporated in the mother (animus), but also from the father's phallus. In this way, Don Juan exemplifies the hinge between the primal Marduk-Tiamat syzygy and the Marduk-Zarpanitu syzygy in the second birth. Nevertheless, it is not quite the symbolic father (which Don Juan will only encounter in the "stone figure" of the assassinated commander) who will hurl him into the funnel of hell. If

Don Juan seeks "Woman in every woman," it is no doubt in order to find there the maternal paradigm; but, paradoxically, he thereby liberates "every woman" from the religious and political tyranny of his time. By scorning them—as much as he scorns himself—this fallen angel reverts to reflecting on himself (*reflecting* in both senses of the word). He is also the hero who tries to save the Virgin (by despoiling nuns), who is subjugated and prostituted by the Monster:

> Prometheus defies Zeus to give power to men;
> Faust, to attain absolute knowledge;
> Don Juan, to attain absolute freedom.

These are the three fundamental themes of Western mythology.

Along with that, Don Juan's constant need to reaffirm that he is not impotent or homosexual is merely a symptom of our whole human condition—its etiology is to be found elsewhere.

Severin, or the Lesbian Man

Severin was feminine like Schreber but did not have any delusions. He was a "woman's whore" like Don Juan, but without the scorn; he desired the masculine in women and loved the feminine in men. He was thirty-seven and an artist, in a domain where the visual plays an important role. He initially came to therapy not for himself, but because of his second wife Anitta. She experienced depression after depression, these aggravated by clastic and autoclastic crises. Anitta's auto- and heterodestructive state cannot really be attributed to her marriage with Severin, which was smothering and sexually unsatisfying. This psychological state predated their marriage, and one can even say that it was a factor in Severin's choosing Anitta. Anyway, by everything about her destructive behavior, Anitta at this point was demanding a final separation from Severin. This separation little by little became obvious verbally, and it was achieved only after a merciless struggle.

But let's start at the beginning. Severin looked physically

like a fresh-faced, aging adolescent: his long curls cascaded onto rounded shoulders, he had a womanly plumpness, a neutral voice, ambiguous mannerisms, and a transparent skin tone that made his lively and piercing blue eyes stand out all the more.

Just one word about his father: "He paid no attention to our education." The mother, on the other hand, had plans for him:

> She always thought that I would become a priest, to the point that for Christmas one year she gave me a priest's panoply—and it was the village priest who had suggested it. Later, she placed me in the small local seminary. It was a huge stone building, massive and cold like a tomb . . . A white-washed dormitory, with white coverlets like shrouds . . . It had a stale, sickly sweet smell, which I have never encountered since. It still gives me the shivers . . .

We won't comment on this episode, except to note the tomblike chill of this phase of his life, imposed on him by his mother "in concert" with the priest. The dreams he remembers are always similar: either he is dressed as a woman, or he is a woman. "Last night again, I was walking around wearing a woman's fur coat."

The reader might have recognized in the pseudonyms I am using for this case the names of Sacher Masoch's characters. Severin especially—and Wanda, who comes on the scene later—is the hero of *Vénus à la fourrure (Venus in Furs)*; Anitta is the heroine of *La Pêcheuse d'âmes (The Fisherwoman of Souls)* and Anna, who we will discuss later, is the heroine of *La Divorcée*. These dreams—and especially the last—are thus very significant.

> I was circumcised when I was twenty-two because of a phimosis which was hampering my erections. From this I still have a very sensitive gland. That was when I met Wanda. I confided in her about my impotence, and she said: "I will prove to you that you are not impotent, you will give me a child . . ." Nevertheless it took me several months to be able to make love to her.

In Masoch this is a recurrent theme: "You are not a man, I will make a man of you," which must be understood as "I will give birth to you again, *parthenogenetically*, without the intervention of a father, in the *hieros gamos* between the Great Mother and the son lover. From this union, a new man will be born, different from the father—whose role, phylogenetically, has not yet made its appearance."[4]

And Severin goes on:

> I was so angry not to be able to make love to her that I cut open my right hand with a knife. Wanda was six years older than me, married and already the mother of two children. I had never told her about my dreams and fantasies of becoming a woman or a transvestite, but yet one day she proposed this to me and I accepted. During this scene she added some excruciating bites and pinches. I managed to get an erection and make love to her—or rather, she managed to make love to me, with her on top. We repeated these scenes and she hurt me more and more; from pins we went on to whips, and the more pain I felt, the more pleasure I got from it. Then my fantasies developed to the point of making me the most degraded possible prostitute. I had dreams where I was sodomized. I still have these dreams and fantasies.
>
> When I was a child (from eight to twelve years old), I spent hours in the fetal position in a box; I was dominated by the material surrounding me, I could no longer move—amazed, I felt an unreal pleasure, a state of physical bliss—at the same time I felt guilty, because I was hiding in order to take pleasure from this situation. It was at that time that I also discovered visual pleasures. Ever since then, images have become for me the way to get away from real life. I have made a career out of it.
>
> About six months after my initiation by Wanda, she introduced me to a world-famous couple who were friends of hers. She had been the man's "lover." We were drinking. X's wife was stroking her husband. Wanda joined her; and I, stricken with nausea, went to throw up in the bathroom. Wanda came and banged on the door. I couldn't open it. Then X and Wanda made love right there, on the other side of the door, so that I wouldn't miss a thing . . . I came out furious, wanting to run away, but X held me back and said to me, "There are things more important than physical love, which is within reach of the lowest mammal—they are friendship and love, which ultimately have nothing to do with it . . ." In short, he convinced me to stay and since then he has become a spiritual father for me . . .

Then the war broke out in Algeria. The separation and life over there were as tomblike as the little seminary from before. Fortunately, I managed to make friends with another unhappy soldier there. This friendship has lasted, unshakeable. I wrote to Wanda twice a day. She answered me, but one day she admitted to me that she had "broken down," that is, she had taken a lover. (I found out later that before this lover, all his friends had "taken a turn.") I got stinking drunk with my friend. I was given leave. Wanda greeted me with her lover and she told us: "I can take on both of you, let's have a threesome; Severin, you are a pederast, you can get yourself fucked by the Greek" (Wanda's new lover, in reality and in *Vénus à la fourrure*). At first I slapped her, but then I gave in. And I felt a delirious pleasure at being sodomized by . . . the Greek/Wanda. We repeated this experience, always with the same delights . . .

As it turned out, the Greek joined me in Algeria a few months later. We wanted to repeat the experience, but it was a disaster. Since then, I have made other attempts to recapture this pleasure, but always in vain. Without Wanda, there is no salvation. I got a bullet wound; fortunately only a flesh wound, in my lower back and buttocks. From this experience I have retained an impression that was undefinable but extraordinary: I thought I was dead for a few seconds. Shortly afterward, Wanda told me we should break up permanently. This didn't prevent her from creating a public scene by scratching my face (the scar is still there) and screaming at the top of her lungs when she first saw me with the woman I had just married, Anna . . . I had thought that with her I could forget Wanda, and I think I would have succeeded, except that sexually I was nearly impotent—I could only make love when a woman took the initiative. So much so that after four years she also dumped me . . .

It was then that I met Anitta, who was very fragile and poetic. She was leaving an asylum where she had stayed after a suicide attempt. I thought that my taste for life would ground her, but no!

Actually Anitta really did need Severin's taste for life, but even more than that she needed a master who would dominate her radically, especially in a sexual way—a Petrucchio capable of taming the shrew that was hiding under that "fragile and poetic" appearance that Severin had first seen in her.

But deep inside himself, did he not ignore the Gorgon who hid within the Siren, waiting for a Heracles who never came?

Just as Schreber prostituted himself for God—and wanted to give birth to God (the syzygic animus of the Great Mother), just as Don Juan provoked the law of God, father of the Horde, so Severin prostituted himself for—and wanted to give birth to—the Great Goddess.

It is surely the Mother's law at work here, what Masoch calls the law of the commune: the matriarchal communities for hunting (Diana, Artemis, the Amazons) and for agriculture (hierophanies of the grain) that populate his works. This Mother's law is parthenogenetic (hierogamic) because the role of the male—of the father—in fertilization was not understood at the time when such law was dominant. The Mother's law provides the space of the first castration, which is imaginary because it has no distance from the body. This distance could not be achieved because the symbolic structures (paternal, through the patriarchy and Father's law) which allowed a mediation and created a distance—especially from the body—had not yet been elaborated.

This Severin did not manage to cross the barrier of his second castration. Masoch's Severin does cross it, in his way, by radically decorporalizing his relationship to Wanda and by demanding—contractually—that she live in a pure, perverse masochism. As for Schreber, he offered himself completely castrated to his God (in the first castration), a God who was persecutory from the beginning. Schreber's greatest desire was to recreate with Him the primal syzygy, in order to give birth to the new world.

As for Don Juan—the Don Juan of Molière with whom we have primarily been occupied—he provokes his God to the point that God inflicts on him the radical castration that is death in eternal damnation. Severin—ours as well as Masoch's—demands from the Mother Goddess a second castration, which necessarily is a new birth. Making him a man means having him be reborn into a new life. Schreber puts the Father at the top of the hierarchy and makes himself his feminine helper deity; Don Juan also puts the Father at the top of the pyramid and provokes him by taking the Mother as his victim, and in this sense he is a pure sadist. Severin, conversely, puts the Mother at the top of the hierarchy and takes the Father instead as his victim, or in any case as the excluded or precluded third. Even the Father is his victim, if we admit that here it is the Father who is "guilty" within the son, and who will be reborn with a new youth and positively validated with him (the case of Hiawatha,[5] of Job, and of Christ, as Jung makes abundantly clear). In this sense, Severin is a pure masochist.

Of course, everyone knows that masochism turns into sadism and sadism into masochism. But we must be sure above all not to confuse these two extremes with what takes place between the two. Between the two, the sadism of masochism (Wanda) has nothing to do with pure sadism (Sade's Juliette, for example) and the masochism of sadism (Sade's Justine, for example) has nothing to do with pure masochism (Severin). In other words, the object—or instrument—of true, perverse masochism will never be a true sadist and the object of true sadism will never be a true masochist. The sadist would never put up with an object who enjoyed his tortures any more than the masochist would put up with an object who enjoyed inflicting them (Deleuze 1971).

Sadism and masochism constitute by definition two worlds that meet at the two extremes, like a spindle of interferences, but which are divided because they spread out toward the protruding center of this spindle. The sadistic world generally belongs to the universe of the masculine principle (not the universe of the man), while the masochistic world belongs to the universe of the feminine principle (not the universe of the woman). The sadist is looking for an institutionalized possession. The masochist is looking for a "contractual alliance" (Deleuze 1971).

Notes

1. See also Freud's analysis of the case, a summary of which is here appended to Schreber's narrative (1955).

2. For Schreber's description of this notion, see p. 49 ff. (1955).

3. As described by Delteil.

4. In the archaic mythologies of the Earth Mother, contemporary with the discovery of agriculture (Mesolithic).

5. An Indian hero from Longfellow's epic. See Jung (1954).

10

A Return to Myth

Abraham, or the Anima of the Father and the Son

The symptom that motivated Abraham, a conservative fifty-year-old, to seek therapy was his son Isaac, a nineteen-year-old student who looks about twelve (four feet, eight inches tall, weighing seventy-seven pounds, prepubescent). Isaac's problems had started six years before with very serious anorexia, and his physical development had stopped at that point. Abraham absolutely could not stand the sight of this "runt," in whom he had placed the greatest hopes of all kinds. He had hoped, for example, that his son would be interested in sports, and he had become the coach of a soccer team for this purpose before his son's illness. Disappointed, disenchanted, mortified, the father could no longer bear to look at this son, who was "unworthy" of him.

Neither could he bear Isaac's mother, his wife, who had always been for him a "mere cavity where children grow." His own mother, on the other hand, who thirty-five years before had been condemned to die of cancer, who was abandoned by her lover when she became pregnant with her son—Abraham—and who was "devoted" to her son body and soul . . . he never abandoned *this* mother, to the point that for the past thirty-five years he had never once failed to have lunch alone with her, without having the courage to make the slightest reference to his father.

> I got married young, because my mother was going to die and I needed to replace her . . . I never thought my wife

could give me a son and that was all I wanted from her. When that son came along, my whole universe changed. The very day of his birth, and every day that followed throughout his entire infancy, I would come home at night and check his weight, deeply troubled that he had not gained as many ounces as usual. There could be no noise, no smoking around him. The slightest "boo-boo" was a major trial . . . But the birth of my daughter didn't change any of that. I was always indifferent to her—but she is growing up well.

In short, a real father hen. Abraham was, and is, his mother's much-adored "honey," and so now he wants his son to be the same way for him.

It took him a long time to discuss his sexual problems:

I have a strange feeling about that. I am much more attracted by womanly things than by a woman herself. The sex act is secondary. When it happens, it is almost against my will. And yet, lots of women attract me.

One in particular troubled him deeply. This affair had taken place six years before, at precisely the time his son became ill. Ingrid, a beautiful eighteen-year-old German student, came to live at the house as a nanny.

She was incredible, the very image of the girl-woman I had always hoped for without ever meeting. I started to love her as I had never loved before. Our affair lasted three months. We corresponded for a while, but her parents forced her to break it off. For six years now I have thought only of her. I even thought she had had a child by me. This year again, I made a long trip in the hope of finding her, but I had the wrong address. I am deeply unhappy that I didn't give up everything for her.

Abraham told me all this without once making the significant connection between this epiphany—external and internal—of the anima Ingrid and his son's illness. When I tried to suggest it to him, he refused to hear. This Ingrid in Abraham's psyche—this Juliet, this Isolde, this adolescent anima, this Kore, daughter of Demeter, this numinal object of the sun demon

(Hades), whose "nymphet" status was only a perversion,[1] this winged grace with whom so many Olympians floundered in Tartarus—she was reborn out of this! This Ingrid-Brunhilde, by her epiphany in Abraham's conscience—although this epiphany is projected (altered) here—had brutally chased away the figure of Abraham's son Isaac (double puer) from his father's psychic space. It was as if Abraham's anima, which up until then had been invested in his mother and his son in a narcissistic *hieros gamos*, was incessantly reborn through them and managed, with each new season, to symbiotically and parasitically acquire a new maturity through Isaac. And then, upon Isaac's entrance into puberty, his father's anima—at last pubescent—had been able to meet his corresponding incarnation, Ingrid. It was as if, by abandoning his son for Ingrid, Abraham had disowned him in his own soul—in favor of his anima, in the etymological sense of "that which animates." Since then, everything in Isaac's growth had been interrupted, since a suicidal anorexic episode—an episode of grief.

What we are dealing with here is clearly a "theft of soul" in the shamanic sense of the term, a literal sacrifice of the son. The one and only dream that Abraham remembered is significant in this way:

> I am in a cavern located in a desert landscape. A torch lights it feebly. At the center, a stone slab forms a table upon which a naked child is lying. A beautiful young woman is standing next to it. She is dressed in animal skins that only halfway cover her. All around, there are men and women dressed the same way, very primitive, many of them crouched down as if in prayer.
>
> Suddenly I am horrified to see the young woman raise an axe above the child's neck. I wake up with a jolt, seized by a profound anguish.

Genesis 22:9-13 (Revised Standard Version) provides an ineluctable parallel:

> Abraham built an altar there, and laid the wood in order, and bound Isaac, his son, and laid him on the altar, upon the wood. Then Abraham put forth his hand, and took the knife to slay his son. But the Angel of God called to him

from heaven, and said . . . "Do not lay a hand on the lad, or do anything to him; for now I know that you fear God, seeing you have not withheld your son, your only son, from me." And Abraham lifted up his eyes, and looked, and behold, behind him was a ram, caught in a thicket by his horns; and Abraham went and took the ram, and offered it up as a burnt offering instead of his son.

Eurydice, the Return of Tiamat-Hathor Through Psychosomatic Illness

Eurydice will teach us much the same lessons as Abraham. In Eurydice's case, everything was not "all for the best in the best of all possible worlds," and Candide would have been disillusioned if he had been a psychotherapist. Eurydice was a forty-five-year-old psychologist with four children who sought an analysis that was half therapeutic and half didactic. This work was half didactic because she helped it along through her own efforts; the analysis had to be half therapeutic because even though she appeared to be doing well psychologically, she nevertheless suffered from rectal colitis. Her illness had not thus far put her life in danger because the attacks of bleeding dysentery were infrequent and not too serious, but they deeply troubled her.

The first problem she brought out was her relationship with her mother. For four years her dreams, fantasies, and rational discussions were organized around this paranoid-schizoid connection to her mother. She described the woman as the bringer of all the world's evils: her mother was at the origin of her bad relationship with her own father, of her unhappy childhood and adolescence, of her difficulty in living certain moments of her own life as a wife and mother, and finally of her colitis. Little by little, through patient listening and through interpretations of certain dreams and behaviors, it occurred to Eurydice that this "trickster mother" was not, in concrete reality, the demon she had been describing. She realized her subjective and intrasubjective part in this aggressor-aggressee relationship. She admitted that this vision of her mother was not exclusively due to her mother's negative ("bad") objectivity, but also that it arose from the negative ("bad") objectivity of her own psychic reality—that is, of the archetype of the destructive mother, of death. She admitted that this objective psychic reality (the side of the O objects) could take the place of objective physical reality (the side of the O′ objects), thus more or less radically veiling objective physical reality from the concrete objective vision of her own mother (a trap of the Imaginary, maya). She thus admitted that no authentic subject was coming to mediate (objectify) this relationship: nothing permitted her to gain enough distance from the objective psychic (archetypal) reality that possessed her and to see the objective physical reality of her mother. She admitted therefore a certain interpretation of objective physical reality, not by her as the subject, but through the possession of her ego by objective psychic reality.

When we talk about subjectivity, or in this case intrasubjectivity, we must be perfectly conscious of the error that we are liable to commit by speaking in these terms. This intrasubjective *subject* is precisely the one that is not a subject but on the contrary the *object* of possession by objective psychic reality (archetypal, O), which does not join with (does not symbolize) objective physical reality (O′). The intrasubjective subject is only capable of creating a third term (the subject, O-O′^{2}) that transcends the two realities and, at this transcendental distance, relativizes them.

Eurydice, after four years of work, thereby managed to achieve this relativization, and that is why her relationship with her real mother apparently leveled off, improved, and even at times achieved a certain harmony.

At that point, the colitis was perfectly healed. In fact, she had been free of attacks for three years, as well as during the three years after she ended her analysis with me (although for "dialectical" reasons she continued with another analyst). At the end of those six years of the remission of her psychosomatic symptom (Solié 1969), however, breast cancer appeared. An operation did not prevent a uterine metastasis, and finally she died after three years.

In fact, by once again reflecting on this treatment with me and with my colleague who treated her after I did, it is possible to see that only the intellect was functioning in our patient. She

111

admitted—of course, intellectually (and that all the more because her studies gave her a predisposition for it)—the most well founded of our interpretations. She sincerely wanted to recognize that her trickster mother was not as negative as she described her and that what she was dealing with was the archetypal Great Mother, devouring and vampiric (Tiamat-Hathor). For all that, her mother did not possess her any less, underneath. The archetypal mother of death (the death wish, in other words) continued her work underground (in a chthonic way). The actual mother could not, in her turn, contradict Tiamat-Hathor and chase her away.

All we could do was to make Eurydice express herself, but in relation to her actual mother, and then give her an intellectual awareness of her "error." But intellectual awareness is not *sym-bolon*, the conjunction of O-O′ and P′-P (and O-P′ with O′-P) that would permit the radical transcendence (intellectual and "sensitive") of this subject-other relationship, establishing her as the subject in relation to an other. The fusion or confusion of the "sensitive" (irrational) and intellectual (rational) areas remained. There was no real other, no real subject. A confusion of the two areas of reality—subjective and objective, psychic and physical—existed at the level of this instinctual paranoid-schizoid relationship to the archaic Mother, and particularly at the level of rivalry concerning the "incorporated penis." In our terms, the animus complement effectively devoured her—and compulsively pushed her to devour the surroundings, toward which she showed herself to be tyrannical in her very hyperprotection.

By exposing her rational (intellectual) mechanisms without bringing in the glue of the irrational mechanisms (sensitive, emotional, affective, instinctual) of consciousness, we only suppressed the sadomasochistic fantasy of death and dismemberment by the Mother (Tiamat). Instead of allowing it, like the animus of Marduk, to create the world (cosmogony) and humanity (anthropogony) through original chaos (*massa confusa*), we only reinforced the original chaos, and finally radically sent her back to this chaos. We favored Tiamat-Kingu (destructive syzygy) to the detriment of Zarpanitu-Marduk (Eurydice's creative syzygy). Like Orpheus the voyeur, we precipitated her into the underworld forever. Wouldn't she have fallen down there despite our "voyeuristic" interventions? No one can say.

But we must realize that in psychotherapy there is no such thing as a harmless intervention.[3]

Notes

1. A reference to Vladimir Nabokov's *Lolita*.
2. But also (O-P') - (O'-P). See the figures above. We are simplifying here by not bringing in the (Oα-P'α) - (O'α-Pα) objects.
3. The oral-anal, paranoid-schizoid fantasy was transposed, exactly as it existed, into her genital sphere. By reversion, the fantasy destroyed the genital at that level; through the intermediary of the cancerous cellular chaos of the genital system, this chaos became the expression of the fantasy.

Works Cited

An asterisk after the title of a work indicates that it is available in French only.

The Ancient Egyptian Book of the Dead. New York: Garrett Publications, 1966.

Avalon, A. 1977. *La Puissance du serpent.** Paris: Devry-Livres.

The Babylonian Genesis: The Story of Creation. A. Heidel, trans. Chicago: University of Chicago Press, 1951.

Bardo Thodol (The Tibetan Book of the Dead). In translation, with commentary by C. G. Jung. Oxford, England: Oxford University Press, 1957.

Bataille, G. 1986. *Erotism: Death and Sensuality.* M. Dalwood, trans. San Francisco: City Lights Books.

Briem, O. E. 1951. *Les sociétés secrètes de mystères.** Paris: Payot.

Champdor, A., trans. 1963. *Le Livre des morts: Papyrus d'Ani, d'Hunnefer, d'Hanhai du British Museum.* Paris: Albin Michel.

Chevrier, P. 1958. *Saint-Exupéry.* Paris: Gallimard.

Chrétien de Troyes. *Perceval or the Story of the Grail.* N. Bryant, trans. Totowa, N.J.: Rowan and Littlefield, 1982.

Corbin, H. 1960. *Avicenna and the Visionary Recital.* New York: Pantheon Books.

_____. 1969. *Creative Imagination in the Sufism of Ibn 'Arabi.* Princeton, N.J.: Princeton University Press.

_____. 1976. *L'Archange empourpré.** Paris: Fayard.

_____. 1977. *Spiritual Body and Celestial Earth: From Mazdean Iran to Shi'ite Iran.* Princeton, N.J.: Princeton University Press.

Deleuze, G. 1971. *Masochism: Coldness and Cruelty* and *Venus in Furs.* J. McNeil, trans. New York: Braziller, 1989.

Fedida, P. 1978. *L'Absence.** Paris: Gallimard.

Freud, S. 1914. From the history of an infantile neurosis. In *SE*, vol. 17. London: The Hogarth Press, 1955.

Garelli, P., and Leibovici, M. 1959. *La Naissance du Monde.** Paris: Seuil. C.N.R.S.

Girard, R. 1977. *Violence and the Sacred.* Baltimore, Md.: Johns Hopkins University Press.

Guy-Gillet, G. 1977. L'image dans le champ jungien. In *Cahiers de Psychologie Jungienne* 14 (ete).

Heidegger, M. 1959. *An Introduction to Metaphysics.* New Haven, Conn.: Yale University Press.

_____. 1962. *Being and Time.* J. Macquarrie, E. Robinson, trans. New York: Harper and Row.

Humbert, E. 1984. Active imagination according to Jung. In *Jung in Modern Perspectives*, R. Papadopoulos, ed. Hounslow: Wilwood House, Ltd.

Husserl, E. 1950. *Idées directrices pour une phénomenologie.** Paris: Gallimard.

James, E. O. 1958. *Myth and Ritual in the Ancient Near East.* New York: Praeger.

Jung, C. G. 1921. *Psychological Types. CW*, vol. 6. Princeton, N.J.: Princeton University Press, 1971.

_____. 1924. Analytical psychology and education: three lectures. In *CW*, vol. 17. Princeton, N.J.: Princeton University Press, 1954.

_____. 1928. The relations between the ego and the unconscious. In *CW*, vol. 7. Princeton, N.J.: Princeton University Press, 1953.

_____. 1946. The psychology of the transference. In *CW*, vol. 16. Princeton, N.J.: Princeton University Press, 1954.

_____. 1954. *Metamorphoses de l'âme et ses symboles.* Geneva, Switzerland: Georg et Cie.

_____. 1961. *Memories, Dreams, Reflections.* New York: Vintage Books, 1965.

_____. 1964. *Man and His Symbols.* New York: Doubleday and Co.

Klein, M. 1975. *The Psychoanalysis of Children.* New York: Dell.

_____. 1984. *Envy and Gratitude.* New York: Free Press.

Kohut, H. 1974. *Le Soi.** Paris: P.U.F.

Kolpaktchi, G., trans. 1979. *The Ancient Egyptian Book of the Dead.* Paris: Stock.

Lacan, J. 1975. *Ecrits*, book 20.* Paris: Seuil.

_____. 1977a. *Ecrits*, selections. New York: Norton.

_____. 1977b. *The Four Fundamental Concepts of Psycho-analysis.* In *Ecrits*, book 11. London: Hogarth Press.

_____. 1988. Seminars. In *Ecrits*, book 1. New York: Norton.

Leroi-Gourhan, A. 1976. *Les religions de la préhistoire.** Paris: P.U.F.

Lévi-Strauss, C. 1963. *Structural Anthropology.* C. Jacobson, B. G. Schoepf, trans. New York: Basic Books.

_____. 1969. *The Elementary Structure of Kinship.* Boston: Beacon Press.

_____. 1983. *The Raw and the Cooked.* J. Weightman, D. Weightman, trans. Chicago: University of Chicago Press.

Levy, G. 1976. Miss Schreber ou la prostituée de Dieu. In *Etudes psychotherapiques* 24 July.

Mayassis, S. *Mystères et Initiations dans la Préhistoire et Protohistoire.* Athens: B.A.O.A., 1961.

Merleau-Ponty, M. 1962. *Phenomenology of Perception.* C. Smith, trans. New York: Humanities Press.

Molière. Don Juan. In *Molière's Dramatic Works,* vol. 2. C. H. Wall, trans. London: Bell and Sons, 1876.

Montrelay, M. 1977. *L'ombre et le Nom, sur la feminité.** Paris: Editions de Minuit.

Neumann, E. 1976. *The Child: Structure and Dynamics of the Nascent Personality.* New York: Harper Colophon Books.

Rossiter, E., trans. *Le Livre des morts: Papyrus egyptiens (1420–1100 B.C.).* Paris: Seghers.

Rostand, E. 1929. *The Last Night of Don Juan.* T. L. Riggs. Yellow Springs, Ohio: Kahoe and Co.

Sartre, J.-P. 1936–1956. *L'imagination.** Paris: P.U.F.

_____. 1940. *L'imaginaire.** Paris: Gallimard.

Schreber, D. P. 1955. *Memoirs of My Nervous Illness.* MacAlpine and Hunter, trans. London: Dawson and Sons.

Solié, P. 1969. *Psychologie analytique et médecine psychosomatique.** Geneva, Switzerland: Mont-Blanc.

_____. 1976. *Medecines initiatiques, aux sources des psychotherapies.* Paris: Epi.

_____. 1980a. *Psychanalyse et imaginal.* Paris: Imago.

_____. 1980b. *La Femme Essentielle, Mythanalyse de la Grand Mère et de ses Fils-Amants.** Paris: Seghers.

Virel, A. 1965. *Histoire de notre Image.** Geneva, Switzerland: Mont-Blanc.

Winnicott, D. H. 1985. *The Maturational Processes and the Facilitating Environment.* London: The Hogarth Press.